St John's

CW01018754

NATURAL RELIEF FROM DEPRESSION

DR NORMAN ROSENTHAL

Thorsons

While the author of this work has made every effort to ensure that the information contained in this book is as accurate and up to date as possible at the time of publication, medical and pharmaceutical knowledge is constantly changing and the application of it to particular circumstances depends on many factors. Therefore it is recommended that readers always consult a qualified medical specialist for individual advice. This book should not be used as an alternative to seeking specialist medical advice, which should be sought before any action is taken. The author and publishers cannot be held responsible for any errors and omissions that may be found in the text, or any actions that may be taken by a reader as a result of any reliance on the information contained in the text, which is taken entirely at the reader's own risk.

Thorsons
An Imprint of HarperCollins*Publishers*
77–85 Fulham Palace Road,
Hammersmith, London W6 8JB

The Thorsons website address is: www.thorsons.com

Published by Thorsons 1998
Revised edition 2000

10 9 8 7 6 5 4 3 2 1

A catalogue record for this book
is available from the British Library

ISBN 0 00 710278 X

Printed in Great Britain by
Martins the Printers Ltd., Berwick upon Tweed

For JEAN

It is hard to describe how great and important the character [of St John's Wort] is and how great it may be in the future.

Paracelsus, 1493–1541

In various patients I have found these effects and, without overstating the herb's benefits, I effected cures which you can achieve neither with all the rest of your Apothecary nor with the best prescriptions made out of gold, silver, coral, pearls, stone or jewels (even those that have been found to be useful and wonderful in the treatment of other illnesses).

Angelo Sala, 1576–1637

After six years of solid depression, of feeling crippled and at the edge of a cliff, ready to jump ... all my ailments have subsided. I no longer feel any need for a medical professional. My faith has been restored. It's a miracle.

Matthew, a St John's Wort user, 1997

Important Note

This book is intended as a resource – a source of up-to-date information about St John's Wort and how to use the herbal remedy in an informed and effective way to overcome depression and enhance the quality of your life.

This book is not intended as a substitute for medical care. Depression can be a serious condition for which a good doctor or therapist is invaluable and sometimes indispensable.

A few recent reports have shown that St John's Wort is capable of reducing the blood levels of other medications that are being taken concurrently. This effect arises from the tendency of St John's Wort to increase the amount of certain enzymes produced by the liver to break down chemicals. The list of drugs that can be affected by this interaction is rather long and includes medications for the treatment of cardiac problems, high blood pressure, seizure disorders and HIV infections, oral contraceptives and hormone replacement therapy (HRT), and medications to prevent rejection of transplanted organs. **If you are considering taking St John's Wort and are on any other medications, be sure to consult your doctor before starting the herb.**

Contents

ST JOHN'S WORT

Part Three: The Herbal Way to Feeling Good: A Practical Guide

Acknowledgements

ST JOHN'S WORT

Thanks and acknowledgement are due to many people, who helped in various stages of the preparation of this book. Jean Carper gave me the idea to write it and helped at each step of the way. Drs Siegfried Kasper, Hans-Peter Volz, David Wheatley and Mueller-Spähn were kind enough to share their clinical experience with me; and Dr Walter Müller for his pharmacological expertise. Dr Alexander Neumeister translated German texts and personally conducted interviews in Germany on my behalf. Drs Thomas Wehr and Jeremy Waletzky gave generously of their ideas and referred patients to me. Dr Kay Redfield Jamison was an inspiration as always. Dr Judith Rapoport, Jerolyn Ross and Helen Wall carefully read and edited the manuscript. Joshua Rosenthal, Stacey Chok and Joanne Milne helped as research assistants. Thanks to my editors at HarperCollins, Gladys Justin Carr and Elissa Altman and to my agent Raphael Sagalyn. My wife, Dr Leora Rosen, gave invaluable support and suggestions. And finally, thanks to the many patients who shared their experiences with the herbal anti-depressant, without whose anonymous contribution this book would not have been possible.

Introduction

If you have suffered from depression, you know the pain and frustration of trying to escape from its black depths. Even if you just have occasional mild attacks of the blues, for example premenstrually or during the dark days of winter, you can appreciate the changes in brain chemistry that bring on the distressing down moods. Of course, drugs to change that brain chemistry are establishment medicine's main way of treating depression.

But now, a new and very exciting drug – not from the major pharmaceutical companies but from Nature's own pharmacy and widely used and researched in Europe – is beginning to make waves. It is St John's Wort, or *Hypericum perforatum*. It is currently available over the counter and a major multi-centre research trial, funded by the US National Institute of Mental Health, is taking place. Results of this study should be available very soon. In the meanwhile, however, there is a tremendous need for information about the herb and its uses, which is not generally available to the public or professionals.

Much of the literature on St John's Wort is in German and is rather technical. In this book, my goal is to provide up-to-date information on what is currently known about St John's Wort and how best to use it, based on the available literature, extensive interviews with European colleagues, direct surveys of many who have used St John's Wort on their own, and my own clinical experience.

If studies in the US confirm European research findings and the public has access to good information about the herbal remedy, St John's Wort can emerge as one of the most popular, effective and safest anti-depressants – even more popular perhaps than conventional anti-depressants. For example, in Germany St John's Wort is the number one anti-depressant prescribed by doctors, far outselling Prozac (by more than 10 times over). Every year German doctors write three million prescriptions for St John's Wort, as compared with 240,000 prescriptions for Prozac. There's no reason to think that St John's Wort will not work on the British fully as well as on Germans. If so, it may become an astonishing alternative or adjunct to the pharmaceutical drugs we now use, and without some of their distressing side-effects.

What Is Unique about St John's Wort?

There are several unique aspects to St John's Wort. First, it is the product of Nature's own apothecary rather than the result of pharmaceutical development. Second, the herb really does appear to work. Third, it has an unusually mild and acceptable side-effect profile; fourth, it appears to have a unique pharmacological action; fifth, it is available over the counter, unlike all other anti-depressants, which require a prescription. And finally, it has an amazing history and mythology, extending back almost 2,000 years. So, paradoxically, the latest anti-depressant is also the first effective medicine ever to have been used in the pharmacological treatment of depression.

It is worth considering each of these unique qualities in turn.

There is tremendous interest in this country in alternative medicine, including the healing powers of herbs – and with good reason. Many conventional medicines originally came from herbs. For example, the heart-boosting drug digitalis was originally extracted from the leaves of the foxglove, and the anti-diarrhoeal medicine atropine from the root of the deadly nightshade plant. More recently we have seen the discovery of the anti-cancer drug tamoxifen, derived from the bark of the Pacific yew tree. So it should not come as a complete surprise that the vast plant kingdom, with its approximately eight million distinct species, should yield an effective anti-depressant as well.

For centuries herbalists and healers from many different cultures have attributed healing powers to a multitude of herbs. Recognizing the need to systematize this wisdom and subject it to some of the scrutiny and rigours of modern science, the German Health Department appointed a group of scientists and medical experts to develop an inventory of herbs for which there was reasonable evidence of some medicinal efficacy. This led to 'Commission E', a report produced in Germany in the mid-1980s which concluded that there was evidence of reasonable efficacy for approximately 300 herbs for the treatment of a variety of conditions. German scientists concluded that one of the most promising of these was St John's Wort, and in the past five to ten years many scientific studies have been devoted to its benefits in the treatment of depression.

To date there have been over two dozen studies of the efficacy of St John's Wort as an anti-depressant, all of them in Europe. I will discuss these later in this book. The simple conclusion to be drawn from these studies, however, is that the herb works. It is a highly effective anti-depressant with a very favourable side-effect profile. Of course, there are questions that remain to be answered with proper scientific studies. How does St John's Wort compare in efficacy and side-effects with the most widely used anti-depressants, Prozac and Lustral? Can this herbal anti-depressant be combined with other anti-depressants to take advantage of their different qualities? What is the best way to switch from a conventional anti-depressant to St John's Wort, and should you consider switching at all? Even though science has not yet provided satisfactory answers to these questions, they are of compelling clinical interest and we need to provide the best answers possible based on the knowledge available to us at this time. I address all these questions in the pages of this book.

The most popular anti-depressants currently on the market, including Prozac and Lustral, are known as selective serotonin reuptake inhibitors, or SSRIs. A great deal of emphasis has been placed on the fact that these medications work rather specifically on the brain chemical or neurotransmitter known as serotonin. This mode of action is more selective than that of the earlier anti-depressants, which affected other neurotransmitters as well as serotonin and consequently produced certain unwanted side-effects. It is now becoming apparent, however, that drugs that act selectively on serotonin can have undesirable side-effects of their own. In addition, other neurotransmitters, most notably norepinephrine and dopamine, may also play a role in the development of depression. Doctors who treat depression frequently seek out medications, either individually or in combination, that influence all three neurotransmitters of interest – serotonin, norepinephrine and dopamine – in order to produce an optimal anti-depressant effect with minimal side-effects. Recent pharmacological studies of St John's Wort suggest that it may affect the transmission of all three of these neurotransmitters and, as such, may have a unique pharmacological profile, which may account for its particular effectiveness in certain individuals.

St John's Wort is now widely available over the counter in exactly the same formulation and with the same level of purity as the German version of the compound. This presents a novel opportunity for those who suffer from depression, many of whom will not find their way to a doctor or be treated appropriately once they get there. But along with this opportunity comes a hazard that must be acknowledged if we are to make the most of this novel development: Self-treatment of depression can be a risky business. It is therefore critical to recognize at what points it really is imperative to seek medical attention.

For the depressed person who would previously not have sought medical help, perhaps out of feelings of shame or fear of stigma, St John's Wort might well be a boon. On the other hand, a seriously depressed person who really needs the wisdom, support and guidance of a skilled psychiatrist may set out to self-medicate unsuccessfully, delay recovery and suffer all manner of setbacks in the process.

In the best of all possible worlds, everyone would have access to a first-rate psychiatrist, someone who would be available, affordable, empathic and knowledgeable, someone who would be there to listen to your sorrows, advise you judiciously and help steer you through all the difficulties that depression presents. Unlike Candide, most of us know that we do not live in the best of all possible worlds. Some people don't have the money to get the help they need and sometimes the help they get is not first rate. My hope is that this book will provide the information necessary to enable the reader to evaluate whether a self-help approach to the treatment of depression makes sense, and to judge when and how to involve a professional in the treatment plan. Sometimes the inclusion of a professional is critical; at other times, perhaps, optional.

It must be acknowledged, though, that many UK psychiatrists do not as yet know very much about the herbal remedy, since all of the research and most of the clinical experience with its use comes from Germany. This situation will presumably change in the years to come, but in the meanwhile the information in this book should be of value to you even if you are in treatment with a professional. An open-minded therapist will appreciate a knowledgeable client. I know that I always do.

One problem with depression is that it can make you feel helpless and powerless. Obtaining knowledge about how you can fight depression is one way of regaining a sense of mastery. As you take each successive step towards combating it, you will begin to turn the problem around and feel increasingly better, closer and closer to recovery. One critical step towards doing that is straightening out the chemical problem that is at the basis of depression. St John's Wort offers a new way of doing just that. As a psychiatrist who has treated hundreds of depressed patients over the years, I have come to appreciate that good treatment of depression is a multifaceted enterprise. It is always useful to combine medical treatments of depression with non-pharmacological approaches; I have devoted one chapter (*An Anti-depressant Lifestyle*) to a discussion of promoting an anti-depressant lifestyle. I believe that the use of St John's Wort — or any anti-depressant — can be greatly augmented by adding other self-care strategies to your treatment regimen.

Finally, it is important to recognize that you may not be able to treat your own depression effectively, even with St John's Wort and the most diligent use of all available self-help strategies. If that should happen it really is critical to get professional help. Depression is a costly and hazardous condition. In the tradition of knowing your adversary, it is worth treating it with respect and mustering all available weaponry against it.

This book is divided into four parts. In the first I tell the stories of various people whose lives have been enhanced by St John's Wort and illustrate the many ways in which this herbal remedy can help conquer depression and other conditions. In the second, I chronicle the history of the herb, from the observations of ancient authorities to the latest available research. In addition I discuss the political and economic implications of the growing use of the herbal anti-depressant. In the third part I provide a practical guide to the use of St John's Wort and help the reader to develop a game plan for using the herb in treating depression, deciding when to consult a doctor, and making the herbal remedy part of an anti-depressant lifestyle. Finally, I answer some of the most frequently asked questions about St John's Wort and its use.

Part Four is a resources section, with useful addresses, suggestions for further reading and other helpful information for the reader.

St John's Wort in Action: Success Stories

PART ONE

It Really Works

Although a common maxim holds that 'seeing is believing,' this statement is actually not always true. Seeing can be quite deceptive, as anyone knows who has witnessed the tricks of a competent magician. Conversely, we believe many things that we do not actually see, for example that the earth revolves around the sun. But in some ways the maxim carries the weight of truth: Those things that we cannot see are hard to believe, which is one reason why they gave poor Galileo such a hard time when he maintained that the sun and not the earth was the centre of the solar system. Similarly, controlled treatment studies can appear quite unconvincing if one doesn't believe in the treatment and the studies are performed by someone else. I encountered this phenomenon after conducting numerous light treatment studies in patients with seasonal affective disorder (SAD), or winter depression. The studies from my group at the National Institute of Mental Health, as well as those of numerous colleagues, told a clear story. Light therapy worked. Yet many psychiatrists who had never treated a single patient with light therapy remained sceptical. On the other hand, the successful treatment of a single patient with this modality was in certain instances more persuasive than all the published data on the topic. So, after studying SAD for several years and treating many hundreds of patients with light therapy, I was amused when an old colleague approached me at a meeting and said to me with an air of discovery, 'You know that light therapy that you have been talking about all this time? I treated a patient with it and the damn thing works.'

In truth, though, it is wonderful to discover a phenomenon for oneself even if it has been described a thousand times before. And so it was for me with the use of St John's Wort in depression. I had read about controlled studies performed in Europe and had actually seen some of the data. Yet it was only when I saw some of my own patients benefit from the herbal remedy that I felt the excitement that might be expected to greet the arrival of a novel form of treatment for an old and nasty adversary – depression.

Fired by a Chemist's Assistant

'This letter is to cancel my appointment,' wrote Malcolm, who worked as an assistant at a chemist's. 'I suppose I could come in and "show myself to the priest" ... but I had only mild to moderate depressions, not leprosy ... I have never been a danger to myself or others, only a danger to my chequebook. And in the interests of protecting my current account, I would like to cancel further appointments.

'I am relatively happy with my current "prescription" of St John's Wort. It is working as well as, or better than, any of the anti-depressants I have tried so far. So I'll keep with it for now, and see how well it does as the days get longer. If I feel the need to try more prescriptions, I will feel free to call.'

Well, I have always encouraged my patients to express themselves freely to me – and apparently Malcolm took me at my word. But his letter captured my attention more for its substance than its style. Malcolm's depression had been very difficult to treat. It was not that his symptoms were so severe. He was correct in describing them as 'mild to moderate' and he had never felt suicidal, but it was long-standing and seemed to sap his life of all joy. His energy level was very low and he withdrew from others in order to conserve his meagre energy reserves for his job. His only pleasure came from buying things, such as compact discs. 'Music seemed to fill my emptiness,' he said. Two women he had dated over the previous 10 years had remarked that his main problem was that he wasn't happy, though he was barely aware of this unhappiness himself.

I had treated Malcolm's symptoms with a comprehensive list of anti-depressant medications, trying each one diligently for the right amount of time, calibrating dosages, using novel and unusual combinations and integrating the medications with all sorts of health-enhancing recommendations. While these interventions were quite helpful, we were always brought up short by side-effects, especially problems with his sinuses, dryness of the mouth and feelings of spaciness. Of all medications we had used, Lustral seemed best but he still felt unhappy and 'out of touch' emotionally. He decided to stop Lustral after finding out about St John's Wort on the World Wide Web and concluded that he felt he had enough information on which to base an intelligent decision.

Malcolm followed his earlier communication to me with a second letter, to reassure me that 'I was in no way displeased with your "psychiatric care" (I guess the term is) and to report on "my current herbal concoction".' He was now on Hypericum 900 mg per day, which appeared both to reduce his anxiety and to energize him. He was 'more positive and upbeat, more apt to say things instead of sitting around and being quiet'. He was amazed to find himself more outgoing and confident, even among strangers. He felt a qualitative difference between the effects of Lustral and those of St John's Wort. While the Lustral had helped his mood, it had not allowed him to communicate that improved mood to others and to engage with them as freely as was now possible.

Over the next six months, while taking St John's Wort, Malcolm made certain changes in his life. He made sure to get enough sleep, which helped his energy level, and kept his time awake constant, even at weekends, which he believed had a marked stabilizing effect on his mood. He left the chemist's, where he had felt isolated, and took up a job in a home for mentally disabled adults, where he had more daily contact with people. He involved himself in religious activities, which added a spiritual dimension to his life. Finally, he plucked up the courage to approach a young woman whom he had met at church and whom he is now dating.

My experience with Malcolm was my first direct encounter with the new herbal anti-depressant, and to say that I was amazed would be an understatement. After treating him with so many potent anti-depressants both individually and in combination and observing his responses to them, I discounted a placebo explanation for his improvement. In his case, I was convinced that the herb had exerted a specific anti-depressant effect. His story reminded me once again, however, how important it is to add healthy activities to any anti-depressant intervention – though again I realized how little these activities help unless the disturbance in brain chemistry has been turned round. I now wonder whether the tendency for St John's Wort to make Malcolm more outgoing might have been related to its effects on the neuro-transmitter dopamine, which is important in modulating social behaviour in animals, while the mood-enhancing effects that he experienced on both Lustral and St John's Wort might have been related to the effects of both of these substances on serotonin.

The lessons I learned from Malcolm encouraged me to try St John's Wort in my own practice. The first patient I treated was Adele, whose story I describe below.

Adele: Lessons from an Anxious Educator

Adele is a woman of approximately 50, whom I have treated for the past eight years. Although extremely intelligent, she has had learning difficulties since childhood – although she has mastered these sufficiently to complete university and graduate school successfully and become an educator herself, teaching others how to teach. Despite the many good things in her life – a loving husband, children of whom she is proud, good looks and physical health – Adele has suffered long stretches of time during which she has felt tired, tearful and, above all, anxious. During these times she loses interest and initiative, has trouble sleeping, is unable to concentrate on her work and devalues herself.

These episodes of depression and anxiety would come and go over the years, sometimes apparently with the seasons, sometimes in response to stress, and sometimes for no good discernible reason at all. And over the years I have treated Adele with a series of anti-depressants, all of which have created problems that, sooner or later, would come to a head so that she would elect to discontinue the medications rather than suffer the side-effects. Prozac caused her to itch unbearably. Wellbutrin made her edgy and irritable. Lustral stripped her of her sex-drive and ability to have orgasms. Light therapy in winter was of some help but not sufficient in itself. Psychotherapy helped her to deal with some of her life issues, many of which were the result of childhood sorrows and traumas, but didn't resolve the symptoms of her underlying depression – fatigue to the point of exhaustion, sadness and, always in the background, all-encompassing anxiety.

After my experience with Malcolm's self-treatment, I finally began to take the European literature on St John's Wort more seriously. I was eager for Adele to try the herb, as her depressive symptoms seemed to fit the profile of those who had most frequently benefited from the drug. I gave her some samples of Jarsin™, the type of St John's Wort used in most of the European research literature and now available under the brand name of Kira™, with instructions based on the advice of my German colleagues. Neither of us could have hoped for a happier outcome. On St John's Wort (300 mg twice a day) Adele began to feel more confident, content and optimistic. Her anxiety disappeared and, best of all, she experienced no side-effects. The return of sexual feelings and the ability to express and enjoy them were extremely welcome developments. Although her job had been a long-standing source of conflict for her, suddenly she felt that it offered her new opportunities which she had not previously appreciated. As far as Adele is concerned, St John's Wort has opened up a whole new world of possibilities for someone who has fought a long and painful battle with depression and anxiety.

Since my work with Adele I have treated numerous patients successfully with St John's Wort and have answered their many questions about the herb. The herb is now widely available to the public and many want to use it but lack the latest information on how to go about doing so. This book is written for all who may be interested in trying the new herbal remedy in the hope that it may lift the clouds of depression and bring joy back into their lives again.

The Prozac of Herbs

ST JOHN'S WORT

We are witnessing a burgeoning of interest in herbal medications, as well as evidence of St John's Wort at work for men and women with a wide variety of different problems and in different situations. Some are taking it on their own, others at the recommendation of herbalists and practitioners of alternative medicine, and yet others, in numbers almost certain to increase, as part of the regimen set out for them by their doctors. What kind of people are using the herbal remedy? What sort of ailments are they treating with it and to what effect? These are some of the questions I have sought to answer in this chapter and the next.

As research has shown, St John's Wort can be effective in the treatment of major depression. Yet, just as with anti-depressants, its use and value very likely extend far beyond the confines of that single clinical syndrome. As the stories in this chapter illustrate, St John's Wort, though mild in its side-effect profile, has powerful and far-reaching beneficial effects which makes it the gentle giant of our herbal pharmacopeia. Its value in the treatment of less severe problems – the heartaches, stresses and ailments of everyday life – are chronicled in the chapter that follows. Although I have changed the names and some identifying details to maintain the privacy of those described, the essential elements of their stories are authentic.

For the benefit of sceptics, perhaps it is fitting that our first story should be that of a man who was successfully treated for his depression without his knowledge. Meet Sam, a depressed solicitor, Sylvia his concerned wife, and her close friend, Louise, a woman of great resourcefulness who happens to be a patient of mine.

St John's Wort in the Breakfast Vitamins: A Single-blind Study

Louise, a professional woman who has been in treatment with me for several years, has in the course of this time become knowledgeable about the administration and regulation of anti-depressant medications and, as a consequence, is much sought after for her opinions in this regard even though she has no formal medical training. Accordingly she was consulted by her friend Sylvia, in connection with Sylvia's husband's difficulties. Sylvia believed that Sam, her husband, was suffering from depression because he seemed 'down in the dumps, sits in front of the television till late at night and self-medicates with junk food — anything he can eat without cooking it; anything that comes in a box, such as our baby's rusks'. In addition, he was having a hard time getting to sleep at night, was staying up till the early hours of the morning and was isolating himself. Sylvia was worried because Sam had previously been a very optimistic person, believing the world essentially to be a good place, full of opportunities, before a series of business reversals had set off these changes in him. She knew that several members on both sides of his family had suffered from depression. When he barricaded himself in the bedroom one night, a highly unusual thing for him to do, Sylvia had reached her limit. It was time to consult Louise.

The idea of suggesting that Sam go to a psychiatrist was completely impractical. 'He doesn't think there is anything wrong with him,' Sylvia explained to me. He would never have gone and wouldn't have considered taking Prozac or any anti-depressant. How might she handle such a refractory patient, she asked Louise in one of their regular phone calls. Louise suggested that Sam try St John's Wort.

The idea was immediately appealing to Sylvia, but certain logistical problems presented themselves. First, she was unable to get her hands on St John's Wort in the small town where they lived, and second she knew Sam to be highly suggestible and she wanted to be sure that he was really better and that she was not dealing with some half-baked placebo effect instead. Louise told her that the first problem could be easily solved, as she herself would send Sylvia the right type of St John's Wort. As to the placebo effect, Louise enquired about Sam's daily activities, and on discovering that he was in the habit of taking vitamins every morning with breakfast, suggested that Sylvia simply inform Sam that the St John's Wort tablets were additional vitamins and add them to the mix. Sylvia approved of the plan. She knew that Sam was generally distracted by work-related matters at breakfast time and, not being by nature a suspicious person, would readily take whatever tablets Sylvia gave him. 'He's lucky I like him,' she observed, adding 'I'm a suspicious person; you could never get away with giving me extra pills.' Nevertheless, she could not push her luck too far and ask him to take vitamins in the evening, which would have constituted a major change in his daily activities and would have elicited suspicion even in a highly trusting husband. In addition, as she noted, 'I have no control over his lunch.' So even though

St John's Wort is supposed to be administered three times a day, Sylvia decided he would have to take all three tablets at breakfast. She knew that the herbal remedy was best taken with food and reckoned that 'if he gets sick, it will be immediate and I will know what caused it.' She was pleased to see that he tolerated the new pills just fine.

After about five to six weeks, Sylvia noticed a remarkable improvement in Sam's mood and demeanour, which she characterized as 'happy but not manic'. He became 'more balanced, grounded, present and alive, better than he has been in years'. He stopped watching as much television, picked up his old musical interests again and spent more time with the baby. In addition, he became 'like a sex machine, morning and night, he was ever-ready.' Every time Sylvia walked into the room 'there was a look in his eye'. She had not seen anything like it in him since they were first married 10 years before.

In fact, Sam was feeling so good that he told Sylvia that he no longer needed the new vitamins. At that point she felt constrained to explain to him why he was feeling so good and why he had better not stop the new vitamins. He took the news like a good sport, and acknowledged that he felt a new lease of positive energy in him. Now he says that he feels so good that he will happily take St John's Wort for the rest of his life, if that's what it takes to stay happy.

Matthew: Finding the Light at the End of the Tunnel

What would you do if you came home one day to find that your wife had left you, had taken your two children with her and had cleared all the furniture out of the house? This is the state of affairs that confronted Matthew one day when he returned home from his job as a security officer. There had been some difficulties in the marriage, but nothing that made Matthew suspect that it was almost over. 'She was so nice to me the night before she left,' he mused wistfully, 'it was as though she was giving me a going-away present.' In fact, his wife had met another man and moved away to live with him, taking the two children with her.

For Matthew the loss was devastating. He had always been a sensitive person. Even as a young boy he had always been 'thin-skinned', feeling more stung than most by ordinary taunts from other boys in the playground. Later, when it came time to date girls, he was always painfully aware when he did not have a girlfriend while others did. 'I was always crushed by rejections,' he recalls 'and would often be disinclined to try things because of fear of failure.' He wondered whether his extreme sensitivity was somehow related to his pale sun-sensitive skin which went along with his ginger hair.

Being abandoned by his wife was one of the biggest blows of Matthew's life. He felt like a failure as a husband and a father and went into a profound depression that was to last six years. During this time he felt like a bad person – if that were not the case, he reasoned, why would his wife have left him for another man? He couldn't sleep at night as his mind 'would race to places I wouldn't want it to go – back to the memories of being abandoned and betrayed by my wife'. During the day, on the other hand, a cloud of exhaustion would overwhelm him when he was at work and should have been attending to the security of the business for which he worked. He recalls how his eyelids 'weighed 1000 pounds each' and he could barely stay awake. He craved junk foods – sweets, donuts, chocolate ice-cream and cakes. His blood sugar became elevated and he needed medications to lower it.

Things became so bad that he felt as though he no longer had any reason to live. Life seemed to lose its meaning and he would ask himself, 'What is this all for?' He went to the doctor for help, mindful that he had proven to be hypersensitive to almost all medications he had been given in the past. The doctor recommended Lustral, but Matthew suffered a serious allergic reaction after only a single dose. His eyes swelled shut, his heart 'raced 100 miles per hour' and he had nightmares and hallucinations.

Shortly after this experience, his mother saw a television programme in which the benefits of St John's Wort were discussed. She suggested that he might try it. Recognizing his sensitivity to medications, Matthew began by taking 300 mg of St John's Wort per day. He felt some relief from the very first day and the improvement continued over the subsequent two months, by which time his depression had lifted completely. His sleep improved and even though he was sleeping fewer hours than he had been, he 'seemed to get more out of it' and felt more rested and alert during the day. His energy level 'was boosted back to its normal level'.

Matthew has returned to his old passion, music, and has begun to play his guitar again. He finds himself walking around the house, singing and dancing. For a long time he'd forgotten that music even existed. Now he is overjoyed to have rediscovered it and will literally burst out into song. He has returned to church again, visiting different denominations to discuss religious ideas with different people. Along with his improved mental condition, Matthew's physical health is also better. Remarkably, given his sensitivity to medicines of all types, Matthew has experienced no side-effects whatsoever on St John's Wort.

Even though his depression is over, Matthew recognizes that he is now faced with having to rebuild his life. 'I am just beginning to see the light at the end of the tunnel,' he observes, 'but I'm not there yet.' He plans to go to the gym and enrol in classes so that he can get a better job. He is even contemplating beginning to date again 'without the old defeated attitude'. He has begun to chat with an old sweetheart from his school days and is thinking of buying some new clothes and taking her out dancing.

He sums up his experiences with St John's Wort as follows:

'After six years of solid depression, of feeling crippled and at the edge of a cliff, ready to jump ... all my ailments have subsided. I no longer feel any need for a medical professional. My faith has been restored. It's a miracle.'

No doctors involved. No side-effects. Complete remission of a chronic and disabling depression. Small wonder, therefore, that Matthew regards St John's Wort as a miracle herb that has given him back his life.

Mercedes: Lifting the Film of Dysthymia

Mercedes is a social worker in her early fifties who makes a distinction between the two different kinds of emotional suffering that she has experienced in the course of her life. The first type, 'the remains of a difficult childhood', took her some time to sort out. But even after being satisfied that she had taken care of the residue of her childhood, she found herself left with 'a light film of dysthymia, which lasted for years and was probably inherited from my parents, both of whom suffered from depression'. Dysthymia is a condition of chronic, persistent low-grade depression.

As a result of her low mood, Mercedes would procrastinate, putting off unpleasant tasks such as housekeeping or paperwork in favour of activities she greatly preferred, such as knitting, crocheting or playing with her birds and her dogs. Naturally introverted, she would withdraw in social situations, where she always felt as though she was holding back.

Mercedes decided to try St John's Wort because it was natural and she understood it to cause few side-effects, starting with 300 mg three times a day. It took at least five weeks to notice an effect, and even then it was subtle though palpable. She stopped procrastinating as much and was more outgoing in social situations. Her husband noted the change, remarking that her dark moodiness had lifted and that she now seemed 'lighter'. She experienced no side-effects whatsoever, plans to continue to take the herbal anti-depressant and is interested in recommending it to several of her clients.

The stories of Matthew and Mercedes illustrate how versatile an anti-depressant St John's Wort is, capable of bringing someone out of the dark depths of despair, as in Matthew's case, or of alleviating the milder and more subtle dysthymia which affected Mercedes. The dosages needed by these two individuals were quite different, with Matthew responding to 300 mg per day while Mercedes used the more conventional 900 mg per day dosing schedule. Optimal dosages of other types of anti-depressant medications vary widely and there is no reason to suppose that this will prove to be different for St John's Wort. The size of the patient is not always a good guide to the best dosage, as these two cases illustrate: Matthew is 6-foot tall and weighs 13 stone, yet required only one-third the dosage used by Mercedes, who is a small woman. Another difference between Matthew and Mercedes is the time scale of the effects of the herbal anti-depressant, from the almost immediate beneficial effects experienced by Matthew to the five-week lag before the treatment kicked in for Mercedes. Such observations indicate why it can be useful to experiment with different dosages for different people and why it is important to persevere for several weeks before declaring a trial of St John's Wort to be a failure.

Fiona: Thinking More Clearly

Fiona is a 60-year-old social worker and mother of three grown children who has been troubled by depression and mood fluctuations for years. Her depressive symptoms have often seemed more physical than emotional. During her depressions she would become fatigued, her arms and legs would feel heavy, her eyelids would begin to droop and she would feel 'rather sad and tired', wanting to sleep much of the time. To some extent these problems might have been related to a condition of adrenal failure, known as Addison's disease, from which Fiona suffers. The steroid replacement that is necessary to control her medical condition has been partly responsible for causing Fiona's mood swings. Because of these mood variations she has never been able to rely on her ability to cope and has chosen not to work at her profession.

Fiona had been on Prozac (20 mg per day) for six or seven years. Although she credits Prozac for lifting her out of her depression, it left her with a 'dazed view of the world'. Things did not feel 'quite real'. Her mind was not clear and she would forget things. Her reactions were delayed and it was hard to keep up with a conversation even though she had previously been an extrovert.

Fiona's GP wondered to what degree her problems with thinking were due to the Prozac, and brought her off the medication in order to find out. She soon became depressed again, at which time he started her on St John's Wort (500–750 mg per day). Within two weeks her mood picked up. Her thinking was clearer and she was able to read again. She rates the anti-depressant effect of the St John's Wort on a par with that of Prozac, but she feels that she is now 'part of the world again'. With her newfound clarity she has restarted therapy and is contacting old friends and having lunch with them. She has even initiated 'play groups for adults', where friends come over simply to do fun things like painting or throwing medicine balls around. These get-togethers remind her of the 'co-operative games of the 1960s'. 'I never got to play them then,' she observes, 'and I want to play them now.'

Memories of Prozac and other SSRIs

Often, in evaluating their experiences with St John's Wort, people such as Matthew and Fiona compare its effects to those of the selective serotonin reuptake inhibitors (SSRIs) they had taken previously. Side-effects of the SSRIs which seem to be less of a problem with St John's Wort include sexual problems, weight gain, diarrhoea, difficulty thinking or remembering and a feeling of being dull or lifeless. Several of the case studies described below illustrate the difference in the quality of some of these side-effects when you compare St John's Wort with the SSRIs.

The comment of one young woman, who had used St John's Wort for the previous nine months to treat her symptoms of depression and anxiety, were typical of many of the responses I received: 'St John's Wort has helped me an incredible amount without producing the side-effects I experienced with Prozac, such as decreased interest in sex and weight gain. It's been a miracle.'

James's Request: Don't 'Prescriptionize' St John's Wort

James, a 50-year-old professional, wrote to me as follows:

> I have had one form or another of depression for over 10 years. My depression has greatly affected my life in many ways. Most notably, my relationship with my wife has suffered and my relationship and reactions to daily work circumstances have been greatly and negatively affected. Many of my attempts to deal with my depression failed.

James describes how he first underwent six months of psychotherapy, which was of no help, followed by a course of Lustral, which helped his depression slightly but caused him chronic diarrhoea, a liability far greater than its minimal benefit in relieving his depression. After he broke his foot, this side-effect became even more inconvenient as he had difficulty getting to the toilet in time. He decided to discontinue the medication and his depression returned with full force.

After doing some research on the herb, James decided to take St John's Wort on his own; within six weeks of starting to take 300 mg three times a day, his feelings of depression began to subside. 'My depression is now manageable and I would have to say almost non-existent,' he concludes. 'I hope St John's Wort remains available without a prescription and that the ... medical professionals do not attempt to "prescriptionize" it ... I hope my short personal history regarding my depression and travels towards St John's Wort will help to keep it available to the general public.'

Better Sex on St John's Wort

Greater enjoyment of sex and improved sexual functioning are among the most commonly reported contrasts between the effects of St John's Wort and those of the selective serotonin reuptake inhibitors (SSRIs) such as Prozac, Lustral and Seroxat. Although the literature on the SSRIs reports very low levels of sexual side-effects (for example, less than 1 per cent for Prozac and 2.5 per cent for Lustral), any clinician who uses these medications will tell you that these figures are grossly underestimated. One survey of patients on SSRIs reported the frequency of such side-effects to be approximately 34 per cent, and it would not surprise me to find an even higher percentage depending on how carefully the patients are questioned. Considering the importance of sex in the lives of many (if not most) people, it is worth considering the difference in the sex lives of people who have switched from an SSRI to St John's Wort.

In some people the sexual side-effects of the SSRIs can be extremely marked. For example, they may cause impotence in men or complete inability to achieve orgasm in women. Depressed people generally have a diminished interest in sex to start with, and any anti-depressant may improve the level of interest and overall drive to connect with others sexually as well as socially by reversing the symptoms of depression. Initially people are so grateful to be free of their depression that any sexual side-effects they might experience might seem like a small price to pay for feeling better. After a while, though, the side-effects become less and less acceptable as they begin to take a toll on a person's relationships and impair one's quality of life.

Sexual side-effects of the SSRIs can involve decreases in sexual interest or arousal or subtle changes in the experience of sex. A colleague of mine, for example, who was previously on Lustral and is now taking St John's Wort, described how on Lustral he had been able to function sexually but the orgasms just did not feel as good. 'On Lustral' he recalls, 'I was still interested in sex and my erections were fine, but it took me longer to reach orgasm and, when I did, the arc of the orgasm was slower and more protracted and did not reach its previously satisfying level of intensity. I am glad to say that on St John's Wort my orgasms are back to normal again.'

It would not surprise me, however, if in the course of time evidence emerges for alterations in sexual functioning on St John's Wort as well, though perhaps only in a very small percentage of those who use the herb. This might be more likely to occur if people push the dosage of the herb above 900 mg per day, as I predict many will in their attempts to explore the full range of the herb's efficacy. I have already encountered two people who claim some alteration in libido and sexual pleasure on St John's Wort, albeit to a lesser degree than on the SSRIs. Given our best understanding, that St John's Wort probably works at least in part by increasing the availability of serotonin, the biological mechanism believed to be responsible for the sexual side-effects of the SSRIs, some sexual side-effects might be expected to be reported as the herbal anti-depressant is more widely used.

It is important to remember that a slight decrease in sexual enjoyment may be an acceptable trade-off in exchange for being free of the painful symptoms of depression. One man whose depression had been successfully treated with Prozac for the previous two years switched to St John's Wort after seeing a television programme about it. Two weeks after the switch he wrote to me that 'the ol' sex drive has come back with a vengeance ... my wife is thrilled.' Several months later, however, I checked up on how he was doing and learned that his depression had returned and that he had developed panic attacks, which resulted in his returning to conventional anti-depressants. It must be acknowledged that no medication, herbal or otherwise, is right for everyone. Nevertheless, St John's Wort may actually turn out also to be of some value in panic disorder, as the following accounts suggest.

Judy: I'm So Excited that I Don't Want to Pull My Hair Out

Judy is a pretty woman of about 30, whose striking features and cascade of straight auburn hair could easily be those of a model whose picture stares out at you from the window of a hair salon as testimony to the hairstylist's skills. What hardly anyone knows is that for about 20 years of her life Judy had been regularly pulling out thousands of her hairs, leaving behind bald patches as wide as golf balls. It was terribly embarrassing for her to look at these bald patches and she would go to great lengths to conceal them with swatches of hair held down with hair grips or hairspray. In school she would stand at the back of the queue so that no one would get too close to her. At the seaside, she would avoid putting her head under water for fear the waves would sweep her hair to the side and expose the source of her embarrassment. Even when she met the man she was ultimately to marry, she resisted showering with him or letting him see the bald spots and, when it was finally impossible to conceal them from him, she told him that they were the result of a bicycling accident.

Judy began to pull her hair out when she was 13 years old, shortly after the death of her beloved grandmother, the person to whom she felt closer than anyone in the world. She felt sad and lonely and unable to talk about it to her family, who were all busy getting on with their own lives. One day during a maths lesson, she found herself pulling at her hair and felt comforted. That was the beginning of her secret addiction.

To add to her problem with hair-pulling, Judy began to suffer from panic attacks when she was 23. These occurred specifically when she went out to eat at restaurants. In the middle of a meal, her heart would start to pound, her hands became sweaty and she was unable to swallow her food. Since dining out was one of her husband's favourite activities, this problem made her very unhappy. She took the anti-anxiety drug Xanax when she went out to dinner, which helped a little, but the panic persisted and she was still unable to enjoy the meal. After a while she began to anticipate with dread the prospect of dinner plans at a fancy restaurant and the persistent fear of having a panic attack felt worse than the panic itself.

Now in her thirties, Judy finally took her problem to a therapist and was given Prozac, a common type of treatment for panic attacks, but it made her feel unpleasantly jittery and she stopped taking it. Her husband's 40th birthday was approaching and they had planned a trip to Bermuda to celebrate. She knew that one of the highlights of the trip for him would be dining out at some of the fine restaurants on the island. She very much wanted to be able to enjoy that with him. At about this time she heard about St John's Wort and decided to give it a try, even though there was no evidence that it was of benefit to people with panic attacks.

Judy started on St John's Wort at a dosage of 300 mg per day, and felt a sense of calm within one day. Since she observed no side-effects, she increased the dosage to 300 mg twice a day for the following five weeks. She and her husband went to Bermuda and, to her amazement, she was able to enjoy going to restaurants for the first time in many years. The panic attacks disappeared and she felt no need for Xanax any longer. Even more amazingly, she no longer had any desire to pull her hair out and she was even willing to show me the patches where fine hairs have begun to grow back again. For the first time in 20 years she has no bald patches that she has to cover or feel embarrassed about. She could barely contain her excitement at the fact that she feels no need to pull her hair out any more, and her eagerness to share her story with fellow-sufferers.

TRICHOTILLOMANIA

Judy's problem of compulsive hair-pulling has a name — trichotillomania. It is surprisingly common among women who, like Judy, frequently conceal it from others by covering the bald spots over with hair. The condition is known to be very hard to treat and anti-depressants, such as the SSRIs, which are so helpful in treating depression, panic disorder, bulimia and obsessive-compulsive disorder, are much less successful in the treatment of trichotillomania. Behavioural strategies to reduce the ease of hair-pulling, such as covering the head with a baseball cap or scarf, putting slippery styling mousse on to make it harder to pull out the hairs, or wearing gloves, may be of some help. But it is an uphill battle for those who are addicted to this activity. If St John's Wort proves to be helpful even in a small percentage of individuals affected by this painful and embarrassing condition, a great deal of suffering will be alleviated.

St John's Wort and Panic Disorder

Aside from Judy's story, I have encountered another person whose panic-disorder symptoms appear to have been helped by St John's Wort. A 25-year-old woman wrote to me from Germany that she had been plagued by episodes of anxiety, palpitations, vertigo, pressure in her chest, tension and irritability – feelings she experienced especially intensely when in crowds and on car journeys. She treated these symptoms with St John's Wort with some success, finding that it helped her to deal better with stress in general as well as with the situations that triggered her anxiety.

Panic disorder is an extremely unpleasant condition characterized by brief but debilitating spells of anxiety, that often come out of the blue and are accompanied by the very physical symptoms this woman reported. During panic attacks, the patient often feels trapped in the throes of a medical emergency and wracked by fears of impending death. Visits to the emergency room invariably yield negative results and a diagnosis of panic disorder is often made at that time. If the panic attacks continue unchecked, anxiety may become chronic as the person anticipates the next onslaught of the disorder. The final step in the progression of the disorder is a reluctance to leave home for fear that an attack will occur in an uncontrollable setting. This last symptom gives this disorder its alternate name – agoraphobia, or fear of venturing into open places.

Thus far there have been no studies of the effects of St John's Wort in panic disorder, but this is yet another condition for which other anti-depressants have proven to be very helpful. Since there appear to be certain pharmacological resemblances between the mode of action of St John's Wort and that of other anti-depressants, there is every reason to predict that the herbal anti-depressant might also work for panic disorder patients, just as it appears to have done for Judy and the young German woman mentioned above. One cautionary note, however, to bear in mind if you are considering using the herb for this condition. Many people with panic disorder are extremely sensitive to all anti-depressants, becoming more anxious and jittery after receiving their first anti-depressant tablets. It is therefore commonplace in using conventional anti-depressants in the treatment of panic disorder to start with very low dosages and move the dosage up very gradually as the patient becomes more able to tolerate the medication. After a while it may be possible to raise the anti-depressant dosage to conventional levels without undue discomfort to the patient. Following these general principles, I would suggest that anyone attempting to treat panic disorder with St John's Wort obtain it in the form of a tincture, start treatment with no more than one-tenth of the recommended number of drops per day, and move up from there (or down if even this low dose feels too much), being guided by levels of side-effects in determining the dosing progression. Once a comfortable therapeutic dosage has been reached, I recommend switching to the Kira™ brand of St John's Wort (see page 203 for more about this).

Adding an SSRI to St John's Wort

Vanessa is a scientist in her mid-forties who has suffered from recurrent depressions for as long as she can remember. During her depressed periods, which can last for months at a time, Vanessa withdraws from others, needs to sleep a great deal of the time, has difficulty concentrating and feels sad and worthless. Although a highly intelligent woman, she lacks confidence in her abilities and for many years worked in a job that was beneath her skills and qualifications. She was reluctant to ask her boss for a promotion, however, as she questioned whether she deserved it and feared that her request would be denied, which would confirm her sense of worthlessness.

In the past, Vanessa was treated with Lustral during the worst parts of her depression, requiring dosages of as much as 150 mg per day in order to obtain therapeutic effects. Although the medication removed the most painful aspects of her depressions, it also sedated her. In addition, she felt that it took away her range of feelings so that she was unable to respond fully to the events in her life, unable to muster great joy in response to good news or feel appropriately sad when bad things happened. As she described it, 'I felt zombified,' and for this reason she would discontinue the medication shortly after emerging from her depression.

Vanessa happened to be in one of her depressions when St John's Wort was becoming widely publicized in the US and she decided to try the herbal remedy at the dosage of 300 mg three times a day. After a few weeks she felt it was helping her – but now, instead of her feelings being flattened out, she felt greater swings in mood than before. Within the same day her mood would fluctuate several times from good humour to despair and discouragement. On the advice of a psychiatrist, Vanessa added Lustral to the mix, trying only 50 mg per day, one-third of the amount that she had previously required. For the first time in her life, she felt good in a sustained way without feeling medicated. As she put it, 'I feel like myself at my best all of the time. I get upset when things go wrong and happy when they go right, but they feel like normal feelings, not depression nor like being a dull zombie.'

Since feeling better, Vanessa has managed to travel and socialize much more freely and happily than had ever previously been possible. She has also plucked up the courage to ask her boss for a promotion, which he readily agreed she deserved and promptly took the necessary steps to make happen.

In another patient of mine, a combination of Prozac and St John's Wort appears promising. The young woman in question wanted to switch from Prozac 20 mg per day to St John's Wort because she had gained weight while on Prozac. Several weeks after the switch she began to feel depressed and we decided to restart her Prozac at a lower dosage of 10 mg per day in conjunction with the St John's Wort. This combination appeared to hold her depressive symptoms in check, but we have yet to see whether it helps her to lose the weight she gained on the higher dose of Prozac.

The lesson to be learned from this young woman and from Vanessa is that one does not have to choose between herbal and pharmaceutical anti-depressants.

The best outcome may come from mixing the two. I would not, however, recommend trying such mixtures on your own, since medications can interact adversely as well as favourably and one is best off having a doctor involved to minimize the chance of that happening.

Switching from a Conventional Anti-depressant to St John's Wort

Considering the buzz surrounding the new herbal anti-depressant, it is likely that many people will choose to try and switch from the conventional anti-depressant they are already taking to the herbal remedy. Let me repeat a few suggested guidelines if you should choose to do so. I would recommend first that you involve your doctor in the process (someone must be prescribing the anti-depressant, after all); second, that you switch gradually, overlapping the two medications in the transition phase; third, that you monitor your progress carefully to ensure that you do not suffer a relapse; and finally, that you be open-minded about returning to your previous treatment sooner rather than later if the exchange does not appear to be working out. The following story of one of my former patients illustrates a successful transition from a conventional to an herbal anti-depressant.

Jake: A Struggling Screenwriter

Jake is a 29 year-old freelance writer and health food shop owner, who is currently trying to write and sell screenplays. He has suffered from feelings of sadness, fatigue and anxiety off and on since the age of three when his parents got divorced. He remembers being sick a lot as a child and getting into many fights at school. He was the class clown and was often in trouble with teachers.

Jake's depressions went undiagnosed until age 22, by which point he felt extremely sad and dejected. He had recently completed his university course but didn't know what he wanted to do with his life. He was working as a fund-raiser for disadvantaged children, but was tired much of the time and had a hard time performing his tasks. When he consulted me that autumn, he had quit work and was home sleeping for most of the time.

Jake had previously been treated with Prozac, but it didn't help his lack of energy, which was one of his main symptoms, and made him feel 'spacey'. I then treated him with another SSRI in high dosages. Although the drug made him feel more energetic and less down-in-the-dumps, it also made him angry and irritable and he developed a nasty edge in his dealings with other people that was quite uncharacteristic for him. To combat these unwelcome effects, I added a second mood-regulating drug, lithium carbonate. In addition, he also received psychotherapy and light therapy. This combination of treatments was quite effective and by the new year Jake had enough energy to acquire two part-time jobs and felt about as good as he could remember ever feeling. He was bothered, however, by medication side-effects such as sleep disturbance and continued aggressive feelings despite the placating effects of lithium.

After several years on this combination, Jake stopped his medications because he wanted to see how he would do without them. He felt fine until he moved to a new city with his girlfriend. He had always had difficulties with transitions and he felt the old familiar fatigue and anxiety coming back to him and consulted a doctor, who restarted Jake on anti-depressants. Once again, he began to feel unpleasantly edgy. At Jake's request, the doctor prescribed a different anti-depressant, Lustral, which helped his mood somewhat but decreased his sex drive a great deal. Not only was he less interested in sex, but also had difficulty with erections and orgasms. He began to avoid sex because it was uncomfortable for him not to be able to perform and affected his self-esteem.

Jake read about St John's Wort in the popular press and coincidentally, I had just begun to treat his mother with the herbal extract with excellent results. Since he is interested in alternative medicines, he put himself on St John's Wort, 300 mg three times a day, and gradually phased out the Lustral. His sex drive, mood and energy improved markedly following the introduction of St John's Wort. The only side-effect was mild indigestion, which responded readily to antacids and was in any case short-lived.

Jake's mood and energy levels are as good as they have ever been and he finally feels 'like a normal person'. He is grateful to the herbal remedy for helping him so much, even though he recognizes that he has also worked very hard to feel better about himself and his life. This work has involved therapy and self-reflection, regular exercise and actively avoiding toxic influences and negative attitudes. He plans to move to Los Angeles where he is more likely to succeed as a screenwriter, and feels optimistic even though his chosen course is a difficult and risky one and he has recently broken up with his girlfriend, with whom he was deeply in love.

Although Jake shifted from Lustral to St John's Wort on his own, it is certainly better to make such changes under a doctor's supervision. But Jake had clearly learned some of the key principles of anti-depressant management during his years of psychiatric care and did a good job with juggling his own medications. He recalled, for example, that you should try not to stop an anti-depressant abruptly if at all possible. To do so is to court withdrawal side-effects, such as dizziness, sleep disruption and flu-like symptoms, to name just a few. Also there can be a rapid decline back into depression again. So Jake was wise to taper his Lustral gradually. In addition, Jake recognized that finding the right anti-depressant is only one aspect of the treatment of depression. He is combining the herbal remedy with other healthy activities, such as therapy, self-reflection, exercise and the avoidance of negative influences. His move to Los Angeles also promises to be a healthy choice for him as it is more likely to offer him the career opportunities he needs in order to feel professionally fulfilled.

Adding St John's Wort to Current Anti-depressant Medications

If one treats a large number of depressed patients, as I do, the use of anti-depressant combinations is standard operating procedure, as the anti-depressants frequently don't work when administered individually. If one has to be depressed, the late 20th century is not such a bad time for it as there is an ever-increasing array of available medications that act on different elements of the neurones responsible for transmitting the signals that regulate our moods. The skilful clinician, working in collaboration with an observant patient, can mix and blend these medications in such a way as to maximize their benefits while minimizing their side-effects.

St John's Wort appears to work very well in combination with all anti-depressants except for the MAOIs, such as Parnate or Nardil, where adding them can be dangerous. This is not to say that medications should be mindlessly shaken into a cocktail in full dosage. After all, if these medications can interact with one another in positive ways that enhance their anti-depressant effects, they also have the potential to enhance one another's side-effects. When mixing medications it is important therefore to move more cautiously with dosages and timing. Certainly, such medication combinations should not be tried on one's own but rather under the supervision of a good doctor.

When properly handled, I have seen people manage to decrease the dosage of anti-depressants that were giving them unpleasant side-effects, and add in St John's Wort instead. For example, Fred, a 52-year-old computer scientist, wrote to tell me that he had added St John's Wort to the anti-depressants he was previously using, which had been helpful in removing his feelings of 'doom and gloom' but did not completely resolve his problems. According to Fred, St John's Wort 'takes the edge off feelings of anxiety and depression and flips the switch from negative to positive'. He was able to reduce his dosage of anti-depressant medication from 450 mg to 300 mg per day and, in addition, noticed that he did not need to be quite so precise as to when he took it. Before starting St John's Wort he had observed that 'If I missed a pill by one or two hours, I'd get very tired and the glass started looking half empty instead of half full. By taking 250 mg of St John's Wort with 150 mg of my usual anti-depressant, I can delay taking the next dose by two to four hours.'

Besides helping Fred get by with less anti-depressant medication and space the pills out at wider intervals, the addition of St John's Wort also gave him a more sustained feeling of well-being. As he put it, 'I feel like good things will happen – a feeling that I am OK – not perfect – but me. I sense life is going to get better.'

I have similarly observed in my own patients the highly beneficial interactions between St John's Wort and other anti-depressants, sometimes subtle, sometimes very robust. Although I have read of people who have experienced problems with such combinations, such as jitteriness or increased blood pressure, to date I have not observed them in my own patients, perhaps because of my practice of altering dosages of medications gradually, which enables one to detect potential problems early before they become too unpleasant.

Many of my patients are on complicated combinations of anti-depressants and I have been pleasantly surprised to find that the addition of St John's Wort may nevertheless provide additional anti-depressant protection even in people with depressions that have been hard to reverse. Sometimes the addition of the herb has been so helpful that it has been possible to decrease the dose of some of the other medications or even to remove one or more of them, thereby simplifying the overall medication regimen. As always, the key to successfully combining medications – and St John's Wort is no exception in this regard – is to change dosages slowly and observe carefully for any untoward effects.

Remember: If you are on a MAOI such as Parnate or Nardil, do not take St John's Wort. Also, if you have discontinued an MAOI, wait at least two weeks before starting St John's Wort.

Combining St John's Wort with Stimulant Medications

There has been a resurgence in the use of stimulant medications, such as Ritalin and Dexedrine, with the increased awareness and recognition of the problem of adult attention deficit disorder (ADD). Since it is not uncommon to find both depression and ADD in the same person, the question will arise as to the safety of combining stimulants with St John's Wort. There is no reason not to do so under a doctor's supervision, using the usual rules of starting low and going slow, as the following two case studies will indicate.

Dick, an economist in his early fifties, was referred to a sleep clinic by his wife, who suspected him of having sleep apnoea because of his snoring. After sleep studies were performed, sleep apnoea was ruled out and instead, he was diagnosed as suffering from narcolepsy, a condition characterized by waking during the night and severe drowsiness during the day. The drowsiness can reach dangerous levels as patients may doze off at the wheel or fall asleep at other inopportune times. Other curious features of this disorder are a tendency to have hallucinations just as one is falling asleep and to collapse while awake, often as part of an emotional response such as laughing. It has been suggested that the dormouse in *Alice in Wonderland* might have been suffering from narcolepsy, as he was always falling asleep and collapsing into the teapot!

Dick's symptoms of narcolepsy were effectively treated with the stimulant Ritalin, but after his drowsiness cleared he realized that he was left with aspects of his personality that he was not happy with, particularly shyness and excessive cautiousness. He would hesitate to initiate conversations, to offer his opinions in group meetings or to assert himself in the workplace. In addition, he continued to overeat and gain weight and his sleep disturbances persisted to some degree. Even though he was not actually depressed and was able to experience pleasure in aspects of his life, his psychiatrist thought he might be suffering from a type of depression and prescribed St John's Wort.

The very day after starting the herb, Dick felt buoyant, which was very surprising to him as he had read that it takes weeks for the herb to exert its effects. He knew that something unusual was going on because he had bicycled into work every day for months and had never before initiated a conversation with one of his fellow bikers. That day he did – and he has been less shy ever since, as well as less self-effacing and more inclined to speak up. Even confrontations which he would have assiduously avoided in the past now no longer seem so daunting. He is contributing more in meetings, feels more engaged and others have noted these changes even more than he has and have pointed them out to him. His psychiatrist has pushed the dosage of St John's Wort higher in an attempt to get the maximum benefit from it. Best of all, Dick has not noticed any side-effects of the herb whatsoever.

I had occasion to combine St John's Wort and stimulants in treating Zack, a 17-year-old boy with a long-standing history of both depression and ADD. When he first came to see me he was on one of the older anti-depressants, nortriptyline. Even though he was on a relatively low dosage of the anti-depressant, he noted a distinct decrease in his interest in girls after starting the medication. 'I am still interested in them up here,' he remarked, pointing in the vicinity of his brain, 'but it doesn't seem to be connected with down there.' This was clearly a case for St John's Wort. In my usual fashion, I gradually added in the herbal anti-depressant while tapering the conventional anti-depressant. On St John's Wort alone, Zack felt too giddy, impulsive and unconstrained, so I reduced the dosage of St John's Wort and reintroduced the nortriptyline at an even lower dosage than before. He declared the mix to be perfect. He no longer felt depressed, was no longer impulsive and experienced a welcome return of his interest in girls both emotionally and physically.

Now it was time for Zack to go off to university, and concentration and focus became major problems, as they invariably are for people with ADD. I introduced Dexedrine 5 mg twice a day to the mix, which helped him with his attention and his studies. He reported no problematic side-effects of the combination and is now enjoying university both socially and intellectually.

While this chapter has portrayed the value of St John's Wort in a variety of conditions that are severe enough to warrant medical attention, the herbal remedy is also being used by countless numbers of people for less major, yet quite disruptive problems of everyday life. Their experiences are discussed in the following chapter.

St John's Wort in Everyday Life

Experience with St John's Wort based on people entering research protocols and seeking help from psychiatrists tells us only about the way the herbal remedy is being used and is working for relatively severe clinical problems. But the large majority of people who have turned to the herb would probably not fit into research protocols nor see fit to consult a psychiatrist. How is St John's Wort being used by the general public, and how is it working for the problems of everyday life? Those are questions that I wanted to answer and realized that in order to do so, I needed to survey the public directly. I did so by means of a questionnaire, distributed in health food shops and pharmacies both in the United States and in Germany, and posted on certain Internet newsgroups. The stories detailed in this chapter are derived largely from responses to this questionnaire, some of which I followed up with telephone interviews.

The St John's Wort Revolution

From the dark realms of cyberspace a 19-year-old girl who calls herself Dream wrote to me as follows:

I began taking St John's Wort for depression – severe mood swings, excessive anger, guilt, feelings of worthlessness and irritability. It helped me function at work. My job requires good customer relations, and I was too easily irritated and hacked off. On St John's Wort I could smile and interact just fine. It caused me a problem only once when I took it on an empty stomach and suffered severe stomach cramps for the rest of the day. I've stopped taking St John's Wort because I feel better now. I was extremely grateful for it because it enabled me to function at work and subsequently keep my job (I recently got promoted, too). I can't afford a therapist or any expensive medications. I only wish St John's Wort worked as well for everyone as it did for me.

Work stress is a common source of frustration in modern times. Perhaps it always has been. But nowadays, corporate downsizing is making many workers increasingly insecure about their jobs. International competition has led to companies trying to get as much from their workers as possible for as little as possible. People shoved into tiny cubicles feel unappreciated and depersonalized. Chronic stress results in both physical and behavioural changes. Physically, there is evidence of increased blood pressure and pulse rate. More stress hormones, such as cortisol, are produced by the adrenal gland, which can reduce appetite and disrupt sleep. After time, individuals can feel burned out and, like the young woman in the above example, can become irritable in ways that can get them into trouble with their supervisors. If stress continues for long enough it can turn into clinical depression and a person would do well to head off such a development at the pass. There are, of course, many things one can do to reduce stress and avoid depression, as outlined in the chapter *An Anti-depressant Lifestyle* (page 166). But one easy solution, which should certainly be considered, is the use of St John's Wort. As in Dream's experience, the need for the herb may be temporary, to tide a person over a particularly stressful time, but the benefits may be permanent. For example, in Dream's case she was promoted, perhaps as a result of her improved mood and better control of her temper while on the herbal remedy.

Although work-related problems are stressful, being made redundant, laid off, downsized or whatever it is called nowadays can be even more so. A 48-year-old man from Germany who has treated himself with St John's Wort for the past year writes, 'I lost my job a year ago. I was finished with the world. Now after a month in a new job, I am fine. With all the problems I was having, I could no longer see light at the end of the tunnel. Now everything is normal again.' There are all sorts of adjustments that need to be made following a job loss and specific actions that need to be taken to determine how best to find new employment or get on with one's career. But putting your brain chemicals in order may be a first step to developing the best mind-set to enable you to make these changes; for this man, St John's Wort appears to have done just that.

Another source of chronic stress is the aftermath of losing a loved one. Grieving is an extremely painful process and probably a valuable and necessary one. Nevertheless, in some people the degree of suffering is so great that some form of medication may be warranted. In one recent study of widows and widowers, researchers found that almost one in four of the bereaved individuals had enough symptoms to be given the diagnosis of full-blown clinical depression. The decision as to whether to alleviate such painful symptoms is obviously a personal one. For many people, the idea of a natural substance, a herbal anti-depressant that they can buy and administer themselves, may prove to be appealing. A 45-year-old woman describes how she has taken St John's Wort three times a day to deal with her feelings of grief following the death of her husband six months ago. She feels that St John's Wort has helped her enormously so that now she is more at peace with herself and can sleep properly again.

The chronic illness of a close relative or friend and the unremitting care and attention this may require is another stress that can wear down those who love the ailing person. One 64-year-old woman felt very stressed as a result of her husband's depression. Taking St John's Wort has helped her enormously without causing any side-effects. Now she feels better and can sleep again.

Although there are no research studies on the use of St John's Wort for the treatment of stress, it is commonplace to recommend conventional anti-depressants for such uses, often to very good effect. Already there are thousands of people using St John's Wort for chronic stress. I predict that its use in this regard will greatly increase over the coming decade.

Subsyndromal Depression

While depression is in itself a common condition — according to one estimate it affects about one in ten people in any given year — many others are affected by depressive symptoms to a degree that would not qualify them for this more serious diagnosis. According to Dr Lewis Judd, former Director of the US National Institute of Mental Health, and colleagues, approximately one in five people interviewed reported suffering from one or more depressive symptom in the preceding month. The commonest of these symptoms are shown in the following table, together with their frequency in the month before the interview.

trouble falling asleep, staying asleep, waking early	34 per cent
feeling tired out all the time	23 per cent
thinking a lot about death	23 per cent
two weeks sad, blue or depressed	12 per cent
increased appetite, gained as much as 2 lb/week	9.5 per cent
decreased interest in sex	9.5 per cent
a lot more trouble concentrating	9 per cent
sleeping too much	8 per cent

If you think about the implications of these figures for a moment, they really are quite staggering. Huge numbers of people are suffering from very distressing problems of mood, behaviour and bodily functions of the type that are associated with depression. Nor are these symptoms benign in terms of their impact on a person's ability to function. Judd and his colleagues found that people with 'subsyndromal depression' reported more difficulties in their work and social relationships than were reported by a control group, and that significantly more people with these symptoms had been on disability. Given the reluctance that people have to seek medical attention even for full-blown cases of depression, and the ill-judged care they might receive once they make such a decision, it seems unlikely that a high percentage of people with subsyndromal depression will be properly treated through conventional medical channels. Such people are therefore excellent candidates for self-treatment with St John's Wort and there is no reason to believe that it will not prove to be helpful for many of them, given its excellent track record in more severely depressed patients.

St John's Wort and Insomnia

As I have noted, insomnia is one of the most commonly reported disturbances in behaviour. As the above table indicates, as many as one in three people reports that in the previous month there has been some problem related to sleep patterns. Many people have written to tell me that they have taken St John's Wort to treat their insomnia and to good effect. For example, a 52-year-old woman began to take St John's Wort 'because I was not sleeping when it was possible to do so'. Since starting St John's Wort 'I don't stay awake if I wake up during the night unless there is an emergency. It also reinforces my positive outlook during the day.'

Although there are no studies of the effects of St John's Wort for insomnia, it is important to remember that sleep difficulties are a cardinal symptom of depression. These difficulties may take the form of having trouble falling asleep, tossing and turning or sleeping fitfully during the night, or waking up too early in the morning. So distressing are such symptoms that they may overwhelm the clinical picture and the depressed person may misdiagnose the condition as insomnia.

All types of anti-depressants may be helpful in reversing insomnia when it is part of the overall picture of depression. St John's Wort is no exception in this regard. People with insomnia might benefit from reading over the symptoms of depression, as outlined in the chapter on *Diagnosing Your Own Depression* (page 131), to determine whether they are suffering from other symptoms of depression as well. If they are, then the herbal remedy is more likely to help resolve their sleep difficulties.

A 56-year-old woman writes to tell me how her sleep difficulties, which were the most troublesome symptoms of her depression, were helped by St John's Wort: 'I can sleep again!' she exclaims. 'Getting rest at night has helped every-thing else; gloom has lifted and I am in good spirits, energetic and positive. I feel a heavy weight *off* me. Immediately (the first night) I began to have dreams. I used to dream lots until about five to six years ago when the menopause kicked in. I did not dream as usual, if at all. I really hadn't thought about it until I took St John's Wort and began to dream again. Maybe the increased dreams are also related to my increased sense of well-being.'

If there are no other symptoms of depression, however, the insomnia may well be due to some other condition. It is worth paying a visit to your GP to have the problem checked out, as some causes of insomnia are potentially dangerous and eminently treatable. One such cause is sleep apnoea, a condition in which people stop breathing for brief spells frequently during the night, which wakes them up repeatedly. This leaves people drowsy and feeling 'hung over' during the day, and puts them at risk when driving or operating machinery. The resulting lack of oxy-gen to the tissues can also be medically harmful. Sleep apnoea is unlikely to respond to St John's Wort, but can readily be treated by other means, such as a special machine that pumps air into the lungs when the person stops breathing.

Simple but important factors worth considering in identifying possible causes of insomnia include commonly used drugs, such as caffeine, nicotine and alcohol. Often cutting down the number of cups of coffee, tea or caffeinated sodas, particularly in the latter part of the day, can work wonders in bringing insomnia under control. Some people may not realize that nicotine is a stimulant and that smoking in the latter part of the night may be preventing them from falling asleep. Even though alcohol has immediate sedative properties, its effects wear off after a few hours. So too much alcohol at night may appear to promote sleep but may actually disrupt it when blood alcohol levels begin to fall. Removing these drugs from the latter part of the day or, at times, altogether, can be very helpful in promoting restful sleep. In addition, sleep experts emphasize the importance of what they call sleep hygiene – a quiet peaceful bedroom with dim lights and low noise levels. They recommend keeping arguments and conflicts out of the bedroom and engaging in peaceful rituals to wind oneself down before bedtime. If such simple remedies don't help overcome sleep difficulties in the absence of depressive symptoms, it is worth seeking out the help of an appropriate doctor. If insomnia is part of a depression, however, it may resolve when treated with St John's Wort or an anti-depressant.

Taking the Edge off PMS

It is estimated that approximately 5 per cent of women of childbearing age have serious mood difficulties during the several days before their periods. Millions more suffer to a lesser degree. Is it possible that St John's Wort might help many of these women feel good all month long? According to some of the responses to my survey, the answer appears to be 'yes'.

One young woman wrote to tell me that she had started the herbal remedy specifically for mood difficulties related to her periods. After six months of treatment with St John's Wort, she now regards her moods as stable, though not perfect. Although she still feels bad at times, she has a sense of being in control of her emotions and that makes all the difference. According to her, St John's Wort has helped 'an incredible amount', without any side-effects whatsoever. A woman colleague similarly informed me that St John's Wort 'took the edge off my PMS symptoms'.

Given the success of St John's Wort as an anti-depressant, these findings of beneficial effects in PMS should come as no surprise, since other anti-depressants have also proven to be helpful in controlling the monthly symptoms of this disorder. Despite the potential payoff of continuous anti-depressant usage in PMS, many of my patients with PMS understandably balk at taking medications and suffering their side-effects all month long to forestall symptoms that persist for only a small (though very unpleasant) portion of the month. Since St John's Wort is very easily tolerated by most people, it may prove to be a boon for such women, who might view it as an innocuous herbal supplement rather than a potent medication with unpleasant side-effects.

Social Phobia

Social phobia, one of the most common hidden causes of distress and anxiety in everyday life, is estimated to affect approximately one in eight adults. People with this problem have a persistent and powerful fear of being scrutinized, evaluated or being judged by others. As you can imagine, this condition results in considerable impairment of functioning as it prevents people from asserting themselves in work or social situations. Although people with this difficulty may simply appear shy to outsiders, actually they spend a great deal of time worrying about being embarrassed, and engaging in painful fantasies of being ridiculed or humiliated.

According to Dr Michael Liebowitz of Columbia University in New York, a pioneering researcher in the field of social phobia, there are several lines of evidence suggesting that brain pathways involving the neurotransmitter dopamine are disturbed in social phobia. To a somewhat lesser extent, pathways involving serotonin also seem to be involved in this condition. Studies indicate that antidepressants may be of some value in the treatment of social phobia. As St John's Wort has been shown to influence both dopamine and serotonin pathways, there is reason to consider that the herbal remedy might be of some benefit in social phobia. As several of the stories in this book have indicated, after starting the herbal remedy a number of people report becoming more outgoing and less shy, and more willing to take the initiative in a social or work situation.

Currently social phobia is a greatly undertreated problem, in part because it is not recognized by clinicians but perhaps also because the very symptoms of the condition – fear of being judged and humiliated – may prevent people from bringing their problem to the attention of a professional. For these people, a herbal remedy that can be purchased over the counter may be enormously appealing. Although formal studies of this use of the herb are needed, early evidence suggests that if you are painfully shy or afraid of making a social overture or asserting yourself, St John's Wort may really be worth a try.

As we can see, there are many possible roles for St John's Wort in everyday life – for stress, low energy, down feelings, insomnia, premenstrual symptoms and painful shyness. Small wonder that the ancients thought this herb capable of miracles, and attributed magical powers to it.

Beating the Winter Blues

Every November, as the days became shorter and daylight began to fade, Sarah, now in her early fifties, would feel an old familiar affliction come over her. An artist, she sees the world in colours. Autumn was a grey season. She would have difficulty waking up in the morning and would sense her energy ebbing away from her. Although normally a competent person, even simple tasks would now feel impossible and preparing for Christmas seemed like a mountainous chore to her. One of her few pleasures was eating — comfort foods such as cheese on toast, scones or buttered toast. She would gain half a stone every winter and lose it again the following summer.

Her depression would deepen in December, made worse by memories of a child she had lost in that month many years before and the departure of her children, who would spend time with her ex-husband during part of the holiday season. The approach of the holidays compounded her misery, making her anxious that she would not be able to celebrate Christmas properly with her two children. At times she was unable to get her Christmas cards out and make all the necessary preparations for the holidays, which would leave her feeling guilty and inadequate as a mother and despairing that things would ever turn out as she wanted them to. She would become reclusive and not want to venture out at all. When she did go out, she would hide in a corner and if someone spoke to her, would nod her head but not really participate. At these times, the world would look completely black to her and at times suicide would beckon to her as a welcome relief from her pain.

Things would improve in January, which was lighter and brighter in part because of the sunlight reflected off the snow, and she found it easier to get through. February, on the other hand, was dark once again and she would only begin to emerge from her depression in a solid and predictable way when March arrived. For the rest of the year she was fine.

Sarah first saw a psychiatrist for treatment of her depression when she was in her twenties. A major factor contributing to her difficulties was the death of her father at age 13 and unresolved feelings around that. Later troubles included the death of a child when she was 31 years old and a 'horrendous' divorce. Despite helpful psychotherapy, her cyclical depressions persisted and she was given anti-depressant medications to deal with them. Unfortunately she was unable to handle any of the synthetic anti-depressants that were tried. Prozac and other medications caused her heart to beat rapidly and did not feel right for her body. She had always been very sensitive to medications of all kinds; even extra-strength paracetamol would make her feel 'high', spacey and giddy.

One type of treatment that helped her a great deal, without any side-effects, was light therapy. She obtained a special light box and would begin to use it from the end of October. She would sit in front of the light, for half an hour in the morning while eating breakfast and half an hour in the evening at dinnertime. The first year she used the light box she managed to get her Christmas cards out on time and was actually able to plan a New Year's party. But even though the light box prevented her from hitting the bottom of her depression, she still felt low and the world still looked dark and grey to her.

About 18 months ago Sarah, who describes herself as 'a child of the 1960s', heard about St John's Wort, which appealed to her because of its herbal nature. She began using it during one of her depressions. Almost immediately she noted a levelling out of her moods and enjoyed not being seesawed by her customary highs and lows. For the sake of convenience, she changed her dosing schedule so that rather than taking the St John's Wort in two lots she took a day's dosage just once in the morning, and found that to work equally well for her. Now she was able to deal with her problems and feel in a stable and upbeat mood, free of depression all year round. She sings the praises of St John's Wort to 'all kinds of people'.

St John's Wort clearly helped Sarah's winter depressions enormously and she was now able to get her cards out early and look forward to the Christmas season. Christmas time, which had formerly been so very difficult for her, now no longer seemed like a black season. She still sits in front of her light box during the winter even though she doesn't feel it is really essential.

Seasonal Affective Disorder (SAD)

Sarah suffers from a typical case of seasonal affective disorder, or SAD. People with this condition are very sensitive to the amounts of environmental light and become depressed when these levels fall below a certain threshold, such as during the short dark days of winter. Although the problem probably has a genetic basis, the severity of winter depressions depends on the amount of light in a susceptible person's environment. Often people with SAD who have lived in different locations report that their problem is worse the further away they live from the equator, with depressions lasting longer and being more severe than when they live in more tropical climes. For some reason not yet understood, women are more susceptible than men to SAD, especially when they are in their reproductive years.

When depressed, people with SAD tend to oversleep. Often they just feel like curling up in bed and being left alone. They empathize with hibernating bears who are free to laze away the winter without the responsibilities that beset us humans all year round. Such responsibilities often overwhelm the person with winter depression, who can barely rouse herself and get going, let alone tackle the chores, work and personal commitments that are part of ordinary living. Overwhelmed by these demands, the person with SAD feels like a failure and anxiety and depression are always close at hand. One source of comfort is often food, especially sweets and starches, which are consumed in great amounts, resulting in unwelcome weight gain.

Seasonal affective disorder is extremely common and has been estimated to affect about 5 per cent of adults. Another 15 per cent are estimated to suffer from a milder form of the condition, subsyndromal SAD or the winter blues. Although most people with the milder version of SAD do not seek out medical attention, the dark short winter days nevertheless interfere with their productivity and creativity and make life feel dreary and dull. It is estimated that approximately one in five people suffers from emotional or behavioural disturbances as a result of the winter.

Light deprivation for any reason will tend to depress these susceptible individuals. Two or three cloudy days in a row, a windowless office or the scarcity of light in their ground-floor flat are all quite likely to lead to a lack of energy and a slump in mood. Once the connection is made between the amount of environmental light and the drops in mood, however, the condition feels immediately less burdensome. As Sarah put it, 'understanding the problem is half the battle'. The other half of the battle can be won with the help of light therapy, St John's Wort and other anti-depressant strategies.

Light Therapy

In the early 1980s my colleagues and I found that the symptoms of winter depression could be greatly alleviated by exposing the SAD sufferer to bright environmental light. Many controlled studies have by now demonstrated beyond question that light therapy is an effective treatment for this condition. Light therapy has been accomplished most successfully by means of special light boxes or fixtures. A typical light box is a square or rectangular metal apparatus that contains fluorescent light tubes behind a plastic diffusing screen. The user generally places it on a flat surface, such as a desk or table top, and sits a certain prescribed distance away from it. In order for light therapy to be effective, the user's eyes must be open, but it is not necessary to stare at the light. Instead, people often choose to read, eat their meals or do anything that can be done while sitting in one place. I used to recommend that people use this time for paperwork or chores, but then I found that they were avoiding doing their light therapy because they associated it with unpleasant matters. So now I advise them to do whatever will succeed in helping them to use their light therapy regularly throughout their winter depressions. Just as with anti-depressant medications, if a person is still in a vulnerable phase, for example during the short dark days of winter, light treatment must be continued even if symptoms are under good control in order to avoid a depressive relapse.

Light boxes may stand upright or be tilted forward, an arrangement that reduces glare and brings the light source closer to the face, resulting in greater amounts of light entering the eyes. Light intensities are measured in units called *lux*. Average indoor lighting is about 500 lux; modern light therapy fixtures result in levels of approximately 10,000 lux, about 20 times as much light as ordinary indoor lighting provides. Properly designed light boxes include special filters that remove potentially harmful ultraviolet rays from the light source. If used as recommended, light therapy appears to be very safe and, out of thousands of people treated with light therapy over the past 15 years, no evidence of any harm to the eyes has been reported. Even so, if you have any history of eye problems you should have your eyes checked out by a qualified professional before initiating light therapy, as some serious conditions of the retina can be exacerbated by exposure to bright environmental light.

The duration of light therapy needed varies with the time of year and the individual, and depends also on what is convenient and feasible. The worst elements of the depression can often be prevented if the problem is tackled early in the season. During the autumn or early winter, just before the usual time of onset of symptoms, it is reasonable to begin with 15 to 30 minutes of light therapy in the morning. Studies have shown that light therapy can be most effective when given in the morning hours, though many people find it to be beneficial no matter when they use it during the course of the day. I therefore often recommend that people start by using light therapy whenever it is most convenient. As the winter deepens, it is often helpful to add a second dose of light (such as 15 to 30 minutes in the evening) to the morning dose. After using light therapy for some time, people often become skilful at calculating how much works for them. Some people require up to 45 minutes of light therapy twice a day in order to obtain optimal effects. This amount of light therapy might seem like a very burdensome time commitment, but it is important to remember that one is often sitting down in one place anyway, and it is often quite convenient and actually pleasant to have the bright, cheerful light of the box shining down on you while you are doing so.

Just as people often learn how much light they need in order to overcome winter's doldrums, so they frequently learn to detect when they are being exposed to too much light. Side-effects of excessive light treatment include feelings of restlessness and overstimulation, headaches or eyestrain. These effects frequently respond to decreasing the duration of light exposure or sitting a little further away from the light fixture. Using light therapy late at night may cause difficulty falling asleep, in which case it often helps to move the light therapy to an earlier hour during the evening or late afternoon.

When spring arrives, people naturally find themselves using their light boxes less and not missing them. But spring tends to be an erratic season and it is prudent to watch out for rainy or cloudy days – especially a string of them – and be ready to bring out the light box at a moment's notice.

An innovation developed to help people who want to move around while receiving their light therapy is a head-mounted light delivery system called a Light Visor. This device is also handy for those who need light therapy while travelling. While many people swear by the benefits of the Light Visor, data from controlled studies of the anti-depressant effects of light therapy are not as convincing for the Light Visor as for the light box.

Simulating the Dawn

Dr Michael Terman from Columbia University originally showed that simulating a summer dawn in the middle of winter could have a salutary effect in people with SAD, helping them to wake up and feel better during the day. He accomplished this by means of a machine that turned the bedroom lights on gradually, as though the shade on the window were becoming gradually brighter as on a sunny morning in the summertime. Since this initial observation, dawn-simulators have become more compact and affordable and have been shown to help people wake up in the morning and have anti-depressant effects in controlled studies. A commonly used version fits easily into the palm of the hand and can be connected to an ordinary bedside lamp. Although not usually sufficient in itself to reverse the symptoms of SAD, a dawn-simulator is an excellent way to get the day off to a brisk start and is a very useful part of the overall programme for managing this condition.

Negative Ions

Another innovation to come out of Terman's department at Columbia is the use of high-dose negative ions – charged air particles emitted from a small device that looks like an air purifier. According to one study, negative ions in high dosages may have anti-depressant effects in SAD patients. More work is warranted, though, before this treatment can be recommended with any degree of confidence. Negative ions are emitted from flowing water under natural circumstances, whereas positive ions are emitted from all sorts of indoor machinery.

Using St John's Wort for SAD

Interestingly, the earliest systematic 20th-century study of the effects of St John's Wort on depression was inspired by the observation that Hypericum is a light-sensitive substance and that rats given Hypericum and then placed in bright light appeared to become more activated. To date there is only one study on the use of St John's Wort in SAD patients. In this study, Dr Siegfried Kasper's group in Vienna compared two groups of 10 SAD patients, one exposed to bright light in the morning for two hours a day for four weeks and one to much dimmer light for the same amount of time. Both groups received St John's Wort 900 mg per day, and both groups responded very well over the four-week interval.

Given the way in which the study was designed, it is difficult to draw definite conclusions from it. Because there was no placebo group, the evidence for a specific effect for St John's Wort was not completely clear-cut. Nevertheless, the anti-depressant results of St John's Wort were promising. In addition, light therapy enhances the effects of the anti-depressant and the anti-depressant cuts down the amount of time needed in front of the light box. There is no reason to suppose that the same beneficial interaction will not occur when it comes to the use of St John's Wort. In my opinion, Sarah's happy experience with using these two treatments in conjunction will prove to be the norm.

There are different ways in which light therapy and St John's Wort can be combined. You could reason that since light therapy is the more established of the two treatments for SAD, it would make sense to begin to use light treatment as you enter the usual season of risk. As soon as it feels as though the light therapy is not fully doing the job, you could then add St John's Wort. Another approach would be to start with St John's Wort and add in light therapy only if it is necessary.

Although Kasper's group found no harmful effects to the eye after four weeks of light therapy used in conjunction with St John's Wort, there is a theoretical concern that the light-sensitizing effects of the herbal anti-depressant may produce harmful effects to the eyes over the long haul. Since such speculations by definition involve watching people over long periods, it will not be possible to answer them definitively for years to come. Even so, it is good to be aware of this possible interaction and to use less light if you are also taking St John's Wort than you would if you were only using the light treatment. This should be easily managed as you will be benefiting from two remedies rather than just one. In addition, we have a natural inclination to do with as little light therapy as is needed to obtain an anti-depressant response.

One tip worth bearing in mind whenever you use an anti-depressant to treat SAD or the winter blues is that the dosage needed usually varies depending on the season. For example, 300 to 600 mg of St John's Wort might be sufficient in the autumn and spring, but larger doses may be necessary to combat the more severe symptoms that may occur in the depths of winter.

How Long Should You Continue?

In general, those who recover spontaneously from their winter depressions during the summer months are able to stop their anti-depressant treatments – be they light or medications – when long sunny days arrive. The same principle should apply to St John's Wort and I would recommend that those who normally feel fine in the summer discontinue the herbal anti-depressant at that time. On the other hand, there are those who feel somewhat down all year round, only more so in the winter. These people are likely to benefit from St John's Wort all year round.

For further information about the effects of the seasons on mood and behaviour, and strategies to deal with the difficulties caused by the short dark days of winter or other forms of light deprivation, I refer the interested reader to my book *Winter Blues* (Guilford Publications, 1993), which deals with these topics in greater detail.

Help for the Elderly

ST JOHN'S WORT

Anti-depressant effects of hypericum have been confirmed in several clinical studies that have compared this compound to placebo as well as to standard anti-depressants ... One of the most important features is that side-effects occur rarely. This benign side-effect profile may make hypericum a particularly attractive choice for treating mild-to-moderate depression in our elderly patients.

Michael Jenike, MD, Editor

Journal of Geriatric Psychiatry and Neurology, 1994

One result of the success of modern medicine in conquering the diseases of childhood and middle life is the ageing of our population and the progressive increase in those of us who can be regarded as elderly, regardless of how we define that term. Depression is very common among the elderly and major depression has been estimated to affect approximately one in seven individuals over age 65 in community settings, and as many as one in four individuals in nursing homes. An index of the severity of this problem is the fact that the highest suicide rates occur among our elderly citizens. The elderly have many reasons to be depressed, including physical ailments, isolation from family, the loss of friends, and financial difficulties, to name just a few. This leads to the common misconception even among healthcare workers that depression may be a natural and justifiable response to an elderly person's life circumstances. Regardless of how adverse a person's life circumstances may be, wherever depression is encountered, including among the elderly, it is certainly worth treating. This will often result in a markedly improved quality of life even though it will not necessarily change the realistic basis for a person's sorrows.

Because St John's Wort has only recently come to the attention of clinicians, doctors have very little experience with its use in older patients with depression. Yet, as Michael Jenike points out in the editorial quoted above, St John's Wort would seem like a very reasonable anti-depressant for those elderly patients who are depressed. As our population ages, medications that are suited to older people will surely become increasingly important and, considering the widespread prevalence of depression in the elderly, it is a particular blessing that Nature's own apothecary appears to have yielded so excellent a remedy for this group of people in the form of St John's Wort.

Perhaps the person with the most experience in treating elderly patients with St John's Wort is Dr Hans-Peter Volz, Chief of the Department of Psychiatry in Jena, Germany. He estimates that he has treated approximately 70 depressed patients over age 65 with St John's Wort in dosages of up to 900 mg per day. He is comfortable with recommending it as a first-line treatment in mildly depressed elderly patients, though he is still inclined to use conventional anti-depressants for those who are moderately or severely depressed. He acknowledges, however, that his practice of not using St John's Wort as a first-line treatment in more seriously depressed cases is not based on any direct experience of its ineffectiveness for such people, but rather on the absence of sufficient controlled study data on St John's Wort in severely affected individuals.

Volz reports excellent anti-depressant effects in the elderly people he has treated with St John's Wort, with very few side-effects. In addition, he has noted no adverse interactions between St John's Wort and the many drugs that elderly people often need to take for ailments accumulated over a lifetime. He emphasizes the need to wait six to eight weeks before passing judgement as to whether the herbal remedy is working or not. Here are two cases from Dr Volz's clinical files.

Greta: No 'Chemical Stuff'

When Greta, a 69-year-old woman referred to Professor Volz by her GP, was asked what was troubling her, depression was the furthest condition from her mind. Instead she complained of many physical ailments — headache, stomach ache, tiredness and an unpleasant taste in her mouth. Her GP had been unable to find any physical explanation for these symptoms and the only abnormality he could detect was a slight problem with cardiac conduction, as measured by EKG. She had complained of sleep difficulties, for which she had been treated with sleeping pills with some success.

When Dr Volz questioned her, it became apparent that her difficulties had begun about two years before, shortly after her husband died unexpectedly of a heart attack. Despite having enough money and a close relationship with her son, who lived in the same town and visited her twice a week, Greta complained of sadness and hopelessness but, she hastened to add, 'only when I am alone'. Dr Volz tried to explain to her that her symptoms might be due to depression, but she vehemently objected to such an explanation. When he suggested that she might benefit from a drug such as Prozac, she refused to take any synthetic anti-depressants, insisting 'that's all chemical stuff'. After two further visits with Dr Volz, he suggested that she might try St John's Wort. To his astonishment, she immediately agreed to take this because 'herbs are not dangerous'.

Dr Volz started Greta on St John's Wort at a dosage of 900 mg per day. He noticed no improvement until she had been on the herbal remedy for six weeks, and it took another 10 weeks before Greta's symptoms were reduced to a significant degree. Greta remains convinced that the improvement she has enjoyed on St John's Wort has nothing to do with relief from depression but rather to 'non-specific' effects of the herb. Dr Volz feels no need to challenge this belief. She is no longer depressed and her mood has been stable without any adverse effects whatsoever – reward enough for a caring doctor.

Success Where Other Medications Had Failed

Anna was 78 when she was first referred to Dr Volz by a local consultant. By that time, her experiences with recurrent episodes of depression went back a quarter of a century. In the early 1980s she was treated with lithium carbonate, which was discontinued when it resulted in thyroid troubles. In the early 1990s she was treated with amitriptyline, one of the older anti-depressants, which caused her severe dry mouth and, on one occasion, an episode of fainting when she got up one night to go to the toilet. Then Prozac (20 mg per day) was tried, and even though it helped her depression to some degree, it caused unbearable sleep problems. Sometimes it would take her as long as two hours to fall asleep at night and then she would wake an average of three times during the course of the night.

When Anna consulted Dr Volz, he judged her to be moderately depressed while on Prozac, scoring 21 points on the well-known Hamilton Depression Rating Scale, on which the higher the score the more depressed the individual. Because of the severe sleep difficulties, Dr Volz decided to switch Anna to St John's Wort. He did this without any overlap between medications, immediately discontinuing her Prozac and starting St John's Wort (900 mg per day). Four days later Anna reported an improvement in the quality of her sleep, but her mood had deteriorated slightly and she now scored 24 on the Hamilton Rating Scale. Her dosage of St John's Wort was increased to 1,800 mg per day. After three weeks her Rating score dropped to 20, after six weeks to 15 and after another four weeks to 10. Anna's depression continues to improve. Once again, St John's Wort triumphed where other medications had failed.

There are several lessons to be learned from Dr Volz and his patients. For many people, like Greta, herbal remedies are simply more acceptable than synthetic drugs. Perhaps it is because we are used to eating plants that they seem more natural than pills do. Even though we need double-blind studies, which include placebo controls, to make sure that any effects of a medication are specific and not just due to a placebo effect, it is hard not to become a believer in the anti-depressant effects of St John's Wort when one encounters patients such as Greta. Adamantly opposed to the very idea that she was depressed and uninformed about the purported anti-depressant effects of St John's Wort, her symptoms nevertheless responded completely, suggesting a specific effect of the herbal anti-depressant. An added advantage of St John's Wort over the older anti-depressants is that, like the SSRIs, it does not appear to have any adverse effect on electrical conduction in the heart. For this reason, Dr Volz felt quite comfortable in using it to treat Greta's depression even though her EKG had revealed some abnormalities in her cardiac conduction.

In Anna's case, we see the importance of persevering with an anti-depressant treatment. After she was switched from Prozac to St John's Wort, she initially appeared to get worse before her slow but progressive improvement over the course of the next several months. Her depression was moderately severe when she first consulted Dr Volz and had apparently been somewhat worse before she started Prozac. Nevertheless, St John's Wort successfully turned it round, indicating once again the potency of the herbal remedy. Despite this potency, the mildness of the herbal anti-depressant was apparent in the ease with which this elderly woman was able to tolerate it in dosages that are very much higher than those widely recommended for the treatment of mild-to-moderate depression. This was in marked contrast with the synthetic anti-depressants she had previously taken and on which she had developed unacceptable side-effects.

A Part of General Practice

In Germany the use of St John's Wort for elderly depressed people is by no means confined to specialists such as Dr Volz. Rather, it is part of ordinary clinical practice, prescribed by family doctors. As part of my attempt to get a picture of usage patterns of St John's Wort in Germany, I distributed my survey questionnaires to pharmacies there and received several replies from elderly users of the herb. My colleague, Dr Alexander Neumeister, a psychiatrist in Vienna, interviewed some of these respondents. Here are three of their stories.

Elsa, a 65-year-old retired nurse, has always regarded herself as an anxious and sorrowful person, never as happy as others. She was treated on and off with the early anti-depressants, but stopped them after a few days because she could not tolerate their side-effects. After her retirement she became markedly depressed and a GP urged her to take St John's Wort. Although she was convinced it would not work, she agreed to do so because it was a herbal extract. Within two weeks of starting the herbal anti-depressant (900 mg per day) she felt her anxiety and depression lift, and is now able to enjoy her life. She spends her time taking care of her grandchildren and going on holiday. She has observed no side-effects.

Irene, an 80-year-old retired schoolteacher, had never suffered depression until three years ago when she developed heart problems. She had several heart attacks and suffered from angina whenever she exercised. She was on medications for high blood pressure. Hospitalized for these problems, she was extremely fearful but regarded these fears as excessive because, as she put it, her life was not at immediate risk and others in hospital were more seriously ill than herself. She had difficulty falling asleep and sleeping through the night, and stopped socializing with friends even though she had previously been a gregarious person. Her doctor prescribed St John's Wort, starting with 300 mg at night. At this low dosage it did not help her, but when he increased the dosage to 900 mg per day, her sleep pattern improved, her depression lifted and she no longer felt anxious. At about the same time she began to feel better physically. She has remained on St John's Wort for three years without suffering any relapse of her depressive symptoms.

Gerda, a 72-year-old housewife, describes herself as a very nervous person with many physical symptoms, especially abdominal pains after eating, for which she has taken medications over the years. She had observed a seasonal pattern to her physical and emotional problems, which became worse during the winter. Six months ago she began to feel so depressed, anxious and irritable that her children took her to a psychiatrist. He initially prescribed Lustral, but she developed feelings of nausea, became more anxious and agitated and stopped the medication after two weeks. On St John's Wort her anxiety has settled down and her abdominal pains have almost disappeared. In addition, she no longer has need for daily pain medications.

There is no reason to believe that St John's Wort will not prove equally effective and well tolerated in elderly individuals in Britain and the US as it has proved in Germany. Even though relatively few older people have taken the herb for depression in the US, here are a few reports that have come to my attention. By now there must certainly be many more such success stories.

Gabrielle: Rediscovering Hope

Gabrielle, aged 62, has had many roles during her life: wife to a foreign diplomat, mother of five, indefatigable fund-raiser for her favourite charities, and formerly a public relations consultant for the fashion industry. But none of these roles prepared her for the role that many of us dread and for which none of us is truly prepared: the role of cancer patient.

In retrospect, warning signs had extended back for many months but, as is often the case, they were missed both by Gabrielle and her doctors. She had previously suffered from colitis, so the typical bowel symptoms of cancer were easily explained away. But after her symptoms had continued for five months, she underwent a colonoscopy and a large tumour of the colon was diagnosed. This was removed at surgery but unfortunately the cancer had already spread to the liver by that time.

Gabrielle had never previously been depressed even though depression runs in her family. Her mother had been affected by the condition, as had three of her four sisters, two of whom spent lengthy stays in psychiatric hospitals and one of whom committed suicide. After the surgery Gabrielle could understand how this third sister had been driven to such a desperate act as she herself was overcome by a 'tremendous' depression. She felt sad and tearful much of the time. Riddled with guilt, she blamed herself for not having attended to the symptoms of her tumour more promptly. She couldn't eat and felt like being sick almost all the time. Normally a very sociable person, she didn't want to talk to anyone or answer the phone. Gabrielle spent much of the day lying in bed, looking at the ceiling. Her legs were heavy and she was unable to walk, which was perhaps just as well because she had thoughts of running into the street and putting an end to it all.

Her doctor prescribed Lustral, which she took for three days but stopped because it suppressed her appetite, made her feel nauseated and interfered with her sleep. Another anti-depressant was prescribed but she was reluctant to take it as it came with warnings against going into the sun and she and her family were on the verge of taking a trip to Puerto Rico to see one of her children. In Puerto Rico Gabrielle's husband told her about St John's Wort and she felt there seemed to be little harm in trying the herbal remedy. Even though the setting was lovely and she was with family, she still felt very down and 'like a drag on everybody'.

Gabrielle bought some St John's Wort in a health food shop in Puerto Rico and began by taking one capsule twice a day. It worked 'like magic' and after a week she felt wonderful. She has been on it now for two months and all symptoms of depression have left even though she needs to go for chemotherapy once a week. 'I go out, I talk to people again and I don't think of my physical illness.' Gabrielle attributes some of her recovery to the loving support of her family and holidays they have taken together, but she is sure that none of this would have been possible without the power of St John's Wort which, to her relief, has been without any side-effects whatsoever. So excited is she about the herb that she suggested that her daughter, who was also depressed, start St John's Wort at the same time as she did. According to Gabrielle, 'my daughter is very happy with its effects'. Gabrielle has been told that the prognosis for her cancer is good and she is determined to live her life as fully as possible. Now that her depression is better she is able to make good on this resolution.

Frieda: A Depressed Pianist

If Gabrielle is convinced that St John's Wort has helped her depression, for Frieda, a 77-year-old concert pianist, the jury is still out on the matter. Her psychiatrist,

Dr Thomas Wehr, is more certain that it has helped with the quality of her sleep at night and wakefulness during the day.

Born in Hungary, Frieda was a child prodigy who learned to play the piano at age two-and-a-half while still in nappies. Seventy-five years later she is still playing the piano, currently in an upscale department store, where she is so popular that families have written to the store management telling them what a treasure they have in her. Not only does she play standard classical and popular music, but also entertains the children with theme songs from their favourite TV programmes. To all outward appearances Frieda is a cheerful person and few would suspect that she is depressed. 'I am a gay depressive, and I don't mean in the sexual sense of the word,' she declares with the dramatic flair one would expect from a concert pianist.

What most people do not know is that Frieda no longer enjoys the many things that used to delight and enchant her. She has withdrawn from people and has not finished reading a book nor been to a concert performance for the past three years. Life feels very difficult. She is pressed for money and everything seems like an effort. Her thoughts often turn to gloomy themes and she is beset by all sorts of imaginary fears. For example, on her recent visit to her GP she worried that she would get lost or trip in his surgery. Even worse, she dwells at times on thoughts of taking an overdose of medications and being done with her suffering once and for all.

Frieda's history with anti-depressants is an unhappy one. She compares herself to an overweight person who has tried a number of diets but has ended up heavier than she was at the beginning. She feels that every anti-depressant she has tried has left her worse off than she was before. She claims to be the first person to give 'a bad report on Prozac'. She can't remember what the problems were with Lustral and Wellbutrin, both of which she tried with untoward effects. She believes Efexor caused 'brain activity while I was asleep – terrifying dreams' that disturbed her nights and left her exhausted during the day.

When St John's Wort began to garner attention in the media, Frieda read up on it in a book of herbs and decided to try it. Frieda discontinued the Efexor and after 10 days shifted to St John's Wort. This is the first anti-depressant she has ever taken that has not troubled her with side-effects. She is highly circumspect about the reason for her improved sleep and energy level, wondering whether it might be due exclusively to being off Efexor as opposed to an effect of the herbal anti-depressant. Her psychiatrist has recommended that she increase the dosage to see whether the improvement continues. In the meanwhile her suicidal ideas have left her and she is guardedly optimistic that further positive developments may follow.

In the stories of the elderly people described here, we see many elements of how depression affects older people. As with Frieda, an actual depressed mood may be lacking in such people. Instead there is a marked *anhedonia*, a loss of pleasure in things that were formerly interesting or joyful activities. Physical symptoms such as difficulty with sleep, appetite or weight changes and low energy levels are common symptoms of depression in older people and are important clues as to the presence of a treatable condition. As we have seen, depression is often masked by many physical symptoms.

Many of the elderly people described here had reasons to be depressed, including bereavement, physical illnesses and the loss of meaningful work. Nevertheless, it is important to treat them medically despite these 'explanations'. Suicidal ideas are all too common in older depressed people and it is critical that these be viewed as symptoms of the illness and not rational responses to life circumstances. Of course it is also important that, aside from medical treatment – whether or not this be with St John's Wort – the nature of these circumstances be understood and that people have the opportunity to discuss them and unburden themselves. Although there is no substitute for the loving support of friends and family, psychotherapy or other forms of counselling can be very helpful in this regard.

There are as yet no formal studies on the use of St John's Wort in the elderly. Indeed, there are far fewer studies of any treatments of depression in the elderly than in younger and healthier populations. As the elderly become statistically and economically a more important demographic group, this situation is sure to be remedied. In the meanwhile, however, the very positive experience of a growing number of doctors and patients with the use of St John's Wort to treat depression in the elderly – its apparent efficacy, ease of combination with other medications and low side-effect levels – is an enormously encouraging development that is surely worth considering for anyone elderly and depressed.

St John's Wort through the Ages: from Ancient Remedy to Herbal Superstar

PART TWO

History and Mythology

For those who are contemplating taking St John's Wort and are worried about its potential for harmful effects, it will no doubt be a comfort to know that the herb has been recommended for therapeutic purposes for almost 2,000 years. But beyond the comfort that comes with history and familiarity, the story of how St John's Wort has emerged from the millions of species that populate the plant kingdom to become a scientifically proven anti-depressant is a fascinating one.

Over the past two millennia, *Hypericum perforatum* has been singled out for its medicinal properties by eminent medical writers throughout the ages, included in the inventories of herbalists and folk healers and the focus of all manner of superstitions. It was only in the last decade, however, that the herb has been subjected to scientific study. In this chapter I will discuss the history and mythology of the herb; a summary of the modern research on St John's Wort appears in the next chapter.

The first person who referred to St John's Wort was Pliny the Elder, a Roman born in Como in the 1st century AD. Although he had a prominent military and political career, Pliny is now best known for his writings, including his famous book on natural history. In this work he refers to *hypericon*, noting 'the seed is of a bracing quality, checks diarrhoea and promotes urine; it is taken with wine for bladder troubles'. A man of enormous intellectual curiosity, Pliny the Elder was ultimately killed by the very trait that was responsible for his great fame: at age 56 he set out to explore the foothills of Mount Vesuvius during the volcano's historical eruption in the 1st century AD and suffocated to death on account of the fumes.

The next mention of St John's Wort is by Diascorides, a Roman army surgeon born in Greece. In his medical text he distinguished the different types of Hypericum and noted that the fruit of this plant smelled of resin and, when bruised, stained the fingers with liquid resembling blood. He recommended drinking the herb with special liquids 'for it expels many choleric excrements ... continually until that they be cured' as well as rubbing it on burns. So well regarded was the herb that it is reported to have been an ingredient of a remedy given to the Emperor Nero in the 1st century AD.

After these two classical authorities, little new was written about St John's Wort for 1400 years, when a towering medical authority of the Renaissance, Paracelsus, turned his attention to the herb. Paracelsus was his adopted name, a bit grandiose in that it suggested that he transcended the earlier Roman medical authority, Celsus, but more user-friendly than his real name, Aureolus Philippus Theophrastus Bombast of Hohenheim. An iconoclastic man, Paracelsus disparaged much of the formal university teachings of the day, wondering in one of his letters how 'the high colleges managed to produce so many high asses. The universities do not teach all things,' he noted, 'so a doctor must seek out old wives, gypsies, sorcerers, wandering tribes, old robbers, and such outlaws and take lessons from them. A doctor must be a traveller.' At one point, as a professor at the

University of Basel, he opened his lectures to the general public as well as to registered students. At another, he burned the books of earlier medical authorities, taking an example no doubt from Martin Luther, who had only a few years earlier burned the Papal Bull. As you can imagine, many were offended by these behaviours. This colourful figure experienced marked fluctuations of fortune and, though fabulously rich and famous during certain phases of his life, he later renounced all worldly possessions and arrived as a beggar and a tramp to minister to victims of the plague in cities where the dreaded disease was raging. He died at age 48.

Among his many medical interests and contributions, Paracelsus turned his attention to herbal remedies, which he regarded as an expression of the will of God. He singled out St John's Wort, which he called *The Perforata*, as a herb of special importance occupying a central place in the totality of God's remedies, which he called the *arcanum*. He wrote of using St John's Wort to treat three separate conditions: wounds, parasites, and what he called *phantasmata*, which appear to be the equivalent of psychotic symptoms, delusions and hallucinations. But he also recommended St John's Wort for healing the soul. Although he mentioned melancholia in his writings, he did not specifically recommend St John's Wort for this condition. It was another scientist, about a century later, who made the first detailed observations about the value of St John's Wort in the treatment of melancholia. The writer, Angelo Sala, credited Paracelsus as his major inspiration, but actually his writings go far beyond those of his predecessor in this regard.

Sala is not as famous as some classical authorities, but he was a very impressive man, surprisingly modern in his belief in the use of chemicals to treat illnesses, including those affecting the mind. He observed in 1630:

St John's Wort has a curious, excellent reputation for the treatment of illnesses of the imagination, which are known by some as phantasmata and by others as mad spirits, and for the treatment of melancholia, anxiety and disturbances of understanding, which sometimes affect highly intelligent people whose primary personality is not melancholic and in whom you do not see persistent melancholic humour. St John's Wort cures these disorders as quick as lightning. It takes a day and a night. With the same power it works against the symptoms caused by witches in a way that is superior — as best I can tell — to the effects of any other type of plant or medication, though these may be very highly respected.

Aside from this being the first clear reference that I can find to the use of St John's Wort as an anti-depressant, Sala's comments are of interest for two other reasons. First, he claims an almost immediate anti-depressant effect for St John's Wort. This is at odds with the experience of many, who have noted that treatment for at least two to three weeks is needed before an anti-depressant effect can be expected. Yet I have certainly encountered individual patients, some of whom are mentioned in earlier chapters, who have noted an immediate anti-depressant effect of the herb. Indeed, if such an immediate effect did not occur at least in some people it is hard to imagine how the herb would ever have been discovered to have anti-depressant properties. Second, it is interesting to note that even though Sala was an enormously gifted clinician, he was nevertheless influenced by the superstitions of the times and apparently believed in the ability of witches to cast their evil spells and in the power of herbs to remove them.

Sala waxes eloquently about the therapeutic effects of the herb:

> In various patients I have found these effects and, without overstating the herb's benefits, I effected cures which you can achieve neither with all the rest of your Apothecary nor with the best prescriptions made out of gold, silver, coral, pearls, stone or jewels (even those that have been found to be useful and wonderful in the treatment of other illnesses). I could not have treated these patients more effectively. I recognize, even as I am describing these cures, that novices who have never had such experiences would be scornful of these claims.

To prepare the Hypericum mixture, Sala recommends that the reader chop the petals and leaves and mix them with brandy; put the mixture in a jar and cover it with a large metal cover; put the jar into a warm water bath; and separate the clear liquid from the sap by decanting it into another glass. He recommends that the prescription be used twice a day, in the morning and evening, for as long as is necessary.

These instructions show that Sala recognized the value of using alcohol to extract the active ingredients of St John's Wort, a process used even to this day in the preparation of Hypericum. Putting the mixture in a warm water bath would make the extraction process more efficient, and placing a metal cover over the mixture would prevent the active ingredients from being broken down by light. Sala's final recommendations – to administer the herbal extract twice a day and to use it as long as is necessary – are in line with modern treatment methods. If one considers that these clinical observations and recommendations were described more than 350 years before the use of Prozac, it is apparent how extraordinary Sala was as a pioneer in the pharmacological treatment of depression.

Before leaving this remarkable man, it is worth considering his attitude towards earlier authorities. He credits them and is highly respectful of their contributions, almost to the point of diminishing his own innovations. But he also emphasizes that it is important to improvise and change the way in which a medication is used in order to make it more potent or effective for a particular condition. In this regard as well, Sala, a little-known 17th-century clinician, showed himself to be remarkably modern and open-minded in his attitudes.

For the three centuries after Sala's writings appeared, the use of Hypericum for the treatment of melancholia was securely incorporated into the German literature, but was remarkably absent in the British and American literature, which stressed the superficial use of the herb for the treatment of burns and wounds. In the early decades of the present century, scientific interest in Hypericum emerged when it became apparent that cattle could develop toxic and sometimes fatal skin reactions after eating large quantities of St John's Wort. Curiously, the skin reactions occurred only on those parts of the hide that were not pigmented, and turned out to be caused by the harmful effect of the sun's rays, which broke Hypericum down into toxic chemicals. Such observations have caused people to question whether toxic reactions to the skin or even the eyes might occur in people who are taking St John's Wort as an anti-depressant. The good news is that there is no evidence that St John's Wort, used in therapeutic dosages, is harmful to either the skin or the eyes. It turns out that cattle develop such toxic skin reactions after eating amounts of the herb that are 50 to 100 times greater than those used therapeutically. Nevertheless, some people do complain of sun sensitivity when on St John's Wort.

The next noteworthy contributor to the history of the anti-depressant effects of St John's Wort, a certain Dr Daniel in Germany, foreshadowed the advent of a modern scientific approach to the herb. Based on experiments with rats, in which he gave the animals Hypericum and exposed them to various intensities of light, which produced both agitation and skin problems, Daniel hypothesized that the psychological effects of Hypericum might be mediated via the skin. He reported in 1939 that Hypericum administered to weakened rats caused them to become more energetic, to eat more and to gain weight. Influenced by the results of these animal experiments, he began giving Hypericum to depressed patients who suffered from loss of appetite and weight, in addition to other depressive symptoms.

Daniel administered liquid extracts of Hypericum three times a day for three weeks to 16 patients with relatively mild depression and observed a favourable response in 12 out of the 16 patients. This encouraged him to use the extract to treat more seriously depressed patients. He particularly selected depressed patients who had been in hospital for several years so that he could feel reasonably certain that any observed recovery would be unlikely to be the result of chance alone. He undertook his treatment studies before the development of double-blind placebo-controlled studies, which are the current gold standard for good clinical research. Nevertheless, the excellence of his clinical observations and descriptions are quite persuasive. Here is an account of one of Daniel's success stories:

A 30-year-old male patient, medically and neurologically healthy, had a nervous breakdown five years ago. Three years ago he missed work over a period of three weeks because of an unexpected state of anxiety. Family history is negative. At present the patient believes that he is a bad human being in that he is not able to fulfil his obligations properly. He ruminates during the night about the following day and is sleeping badly. He tried sleep medications (valerian). In the past two weeks he had no appetite and lost weight. He is crying a lot and has suicidal thoughts.

The diagnosis is reactive depression. The treatment is a vegetarian diet without salt and hydrotherapy, with extract of Hypericum, 5 drops three times a day. On the third day of treatment there is a very obvious deterioration of his condition and then he expresses suicidal intentions. The dose is increased to 6 drops three times a day and on the fifth day of this regimen there is a slight improvement in his condition. His dosage is increased further to 7 drops three times a day and on the tenth day of this regimen there is a marked desire to eat and spontaneous sleep. His suppressed self is freed up and 14 days after beginning the treatment he eats enough on a regular basis, sleeps every night for six hours, feels, as the patient himself describes it, 'completely changed' and wants to be discharged. This is done after another week when the patient reports being free of all feelings of guilt, strong enough, happy to go to work, and healthy in body and in mind. In addition, there are no objective signs of any depressive symptoms.

Daniel reported eight similar cases with similar responses to Hypericum. He observed no relapses in these patients over the course of a year, during which they continued to work and felt fully recovered. Daniel was by no means indiscriminate in his positive reports on Hypericum. In contrast to his experience in the treatment of depression, he noted no beneficial effects of Hypericum in the treatment of schizophrenia, nor in the type of Parkinsonism which followed the severe flu epidemic (*encephalitis lethargica*) as discussed by Oliver Sacks in his popular book *Awakenings*. Daniel hypothesized that the anti-depressant effects of Hypericum were mediated via the effects of light absorbed through the skin and acting on circulating Hypericum and blood-borne pigments. Nevertheless, he acknowledged that this was all speculative and emphasized the practical importance of bringing the beneficial effects of Hypericum to the reader's attention regardless of the mechanism by which these effects were mediated.

I report the writings of Daniel in detail because in many ways he was surprisingly modern in his approach, moving from animal experiments to human studies, documenting his cases with clarity, testing an hypothesis and reaching useful conclusions. His case notes are remarkably well written, comprehensive yet succinct. His practice of gradually increasing the dosage of Hypericum is right in line with good modern anti-depressant treatment and his dosing regimen – three times a day for three weeks – is identical to that recommended for modern treatment with St John's Wort and employed in many of the modern treatment studies described in the next chapter. One noteworthy point in the above description of the depressed young man is that Daniel persisted with his treatment despite an apparent initial setback, recognizing that a favourable response to anti-depressant treatment does not always involve a linear improvement from day one. No doubt the advent of the Second World War caused Daniel's clinical research – and that of many other German scientists – to lie buried in the history books. It was to take another half-century before Hypericum would once again be studied in such a systematic way and, once again, this would occur in Germany.

Fuga daemonum: The Devil's Scourge

Formerly it was supposed, and not without reason, that madmen were possessed of the devil, and this plant was found so successful in that disorder, that it had the title of Fuga daemonum, as curing demoniacs.

Robert John Thornton, 1814

St John's Wort, St John's Wort,
My envy whosoever has thee,
I will pluck thee with my right hand
I will preserve thee with my left hand,
Who so findeth thee in the cattlefold,
Shall never be without kine.

Carmichael, 1900

For centuries St John's Wort has been the focus of innumerable superstitions. It comes into bloom around 24th June, St John's Day, and perhaps for this reason has been named after the saint both in the English-speaking world and in Germany, where it is called *Johanniskraut*. Its spotted petals when rubbed between the fingers yield a red liquid said to be reminiscent of the blood of the martyred saint. With its crown of yellow petals and its delicate yellow ray-like filaments, it readily conjures up associations with the sun, which are reinforced by the appearance of its flowers so close to the summer solstice.

In general, St John's Wort has been used to ward off evil spirits, a practice that goes back to the time of the ancient Greeks and Romans. Some consider the very word hypericon to be derived from two Greek words, *hyper* (above) and *eikon* (image), indicating its power over apparitions or spirits. This 'devil-busting' property was formalized in one of the earliest compendiums of drugs, the Salternitan Drug List of the 13th century, which referred to St John's Wort as *herba demonis fuga*, or the herb that chases away the devil. From that time onwards its magical properties were frequently noted and an official medical textbook of the 16th century, the *New Kreuterbuch*, referred to St John's Wort as *Fuga demonum* or the Devil's Scourge, a term that was repeated frequently in the literature over the next several hundred years. It is tempting to speculate that the anti-depressant effects of the herb might have inspired some of these superstitions, given the ignorance about mental illness that abounded over those centuries. If mental illness was the result of demonic possession, surely anything that cured it must be a charm against the devil?

Franciscan monks used the herb in their exorcism rituals in the 17th century, and ordinary people would carry the herb around with them as a talisman. Even Paracelsus and Sala, whose medical writings were so impressive, recommended that people wear the herb in their shirts or under their hats to ward off the spirits that were thought to cause madness. Children wove the herb into garlands and threw them on the roofs of houses to safeguard their inhabitants. The herb was known as a 'Love Oracle' which could predict the fate of a love affair. Women would press the buds between their fingers, think of their loved one and see whether the sap that oozed out of the plant was red or colourless. While doing so, they would chant: 'If my lover's good, the blood will run red; if my lover's gone, there'll be only foam.' Others would use the plant to determine which member of the family would live the longest. Some believed it would repel thunderstorms. Women carried the herb on their bodies to keep lusty men at bay and it was supposed to be especially good for warding off a demon lover. Yet others used it to detect if a witch had entered a house (in which case the plant would, it was said, wilt) or to induce a witch to declare herself. According to one myth, the devil was so angry at the herb's magical powers that he penetrated its leaves with needles, thereby explaining the origin of their perforations. The list of superstitions goes on and on.

These superstitions knew no geographic boundaries and they were rampant throughout Europe and the British Isles. One British account of the magical powers of Hypericum appears in John Aubrey's *Miscellanies*, published in 1696:

> A House (or Chamber) somewhere in London was Haunted; the
> Curtains would be rashed at Night, and awake the Gentleman that lay

there, who was Musical and a familiar acquaintance of Henry Louis. Henry Louis to be satisfied did lie with him; and the Curtains were rashed so then: The Gentleman grew lean and pale with the frights, One Dr _____ Cured the House of this disturbance and Mr Louis said that the principal ingredient was Hypericon put under his Pillow.

Some people will stop at nothing in their quest for scientific truth.

Not everyone went along with these superstitions. Since a number of the herbalists who recommended St John's Wort for its magical properties were women, and since many of those in the church or medical profession who disapproved of these practices were men, the scepticism of these men sometimes took on a misogynist edge. This is evident in the title of an early 18th-century book on superstitions, 'The Philosophy of the Shining Skirts or The Accurate Investigation of Superstitions Performed by Many Women of Supernatural Brilliance'. A similar tone is struck by the following poem, written by a priest at the end of the 16th century:

Hard Hay is the name of the herb
Usually you find it in very dry places
It's called Johanniskraut or Fuga Demonum
It's superstition and nonsense
Women herbalists who deal extensively in such matters
Should be penalized as soon as possible
So abandon such superstitions
And don't try to save money by avoiding the doctor

As we arrive at the beginning of the 21th century, it is as important as ever to separate fact from fancy and science from mythology. In addition, the question of whether simply to go ahead and take St John's Wort on one's own or to consult a doctor is as relevant now as it was to the 16th-century priest who wrote the poem quoted above. Should you go into the chemist's and treat yourself with St John's Wort, or should you instead go to the doctor? There are those who have a vested interest in your following one course of action or another. In later chapters I will discuss the latest scientific research on St John's Wort, as well as the politics and economics of St John's Wort and when it really does pay to consult a doctor.

Modern Times:
Research Findings

Even though research is still going on, the available data show that Hypericum extract is clinically effective as an anti-depressant drug and that it probably works by biochemical mechanisms not so much different from the mechanisms of action of the tricyclics or the SSRIs. We feel that these findings are important enough to be communicated and interesting enough to stimulate further research.

Walter E. Müller, Frankfurt

Siegfried Kasper, Vienna 1997

The modern era of research into St John's Wort was ushered in by the German Health Department, which set up Commission E to investigate the many herbal remedies in general use in Germany and to find out for which of these there was reasonable evidence of efficacy. Commission E came out with its report in 1984 and identified approximately 300 herbs for which such evidence existed. Shortly after this, certain German pharmaceutical companies targeted some of these herbs as worthy of particular research attention; St John's Wort was one of these herbs.

Research into a new treatment, such as St John's Wort for depression, usually develops in predictable ways. One needs to establish whether the treatment actually works, who benefits most from it, what dosages are appropriate and for how long treatment should be continued. Side-effects need to be documented. Only once a treatment is regarded as safe and effective does attention usually turn to how the treatment actually works. Research in St John's Wort is ongoing, but so far it has taken these expected directions. In this chapter I summarize the state of the art of research on the herbal anti-depressant.

Is St John's Wort an Effective Anti-depressant?

The only studies of efficacy of St John's Wort conducted to date have been done in Europe. These studies came to the attention of the US medical community initially when an issue of the *Journal of Geriatric Psychiatry and Neurology* was devoted to Hypericum in 1994 and later, when the highly regarded *British Medical Journal* published a meta-analysis of randomized clinical trials of the herbal remedy. In a meta-analysis, several small studies are combined together in order to determine whether certain general conclusions can be derived from the data obtained from them.

In their meta-analysis, Linde and colleagues addressed three simple questions: Is Hypericum more effective than placebo? Is it as effective as standard anti-depressant treatments? And does it have fewer side-effects than standard anti-depressant treatments? In order to increase their chances of reaching valid conclusions, these researchers included in their meta-analysis only those studies that randomly assigned patients to different treatment conditions, which is generally regarded as a prerequisite for a valid clinical trial. It would not be valid, for example, to assign severely depressed patients one type of treatment and mildly depressed patients another. These researchers also used state-of-the art statistical methods to compare the treatment interventions.

Interestingly, when Linde and colleagues used only conventional computerized searches of the medical literature, they located fewer than a third of those clinical trials that they ultimately chose to include. This reflects the division separating herbal and conventional medicine which has been so prominent until recently and which persists to some extent even at the present time. Almost all studies were published in languages other than English, reflecting the fact that the recent development of herbal medicine has come predominantly from the German-speaking world. Finally, the authors had to go through many revisions before the prestigious mainstream *British Medical Journal* was willing to publish the review.

Altogether the authors analysed 23 randomized trials involving 1,757 patients suffering from mild to moderate depressions. In 13 trials of Hypericum versus placebo, Linde and colleagues found Hypericum to be clearly superior to placebo, yielding a response rate of 55 per cent as compared with 22 per cent for the control placebo treatment. In three trials of Hypericum versus stand-ard anti-depressants, the two treatments were very similar, possibly favouring Hypericum. But when side-effects were compared, Hypericum emerged as the clear winner, with approximately 20 per cent of the Hypericum group reporting side-effects, as compared with about 53 per cent of those taking standard anti-depressants. Several studies reviewed by the researchers used combinations of

St John's Wort and valerian, an herbal sedative. I have excluded those studies from the present discussion, though their results were consistent with those which used St John's Wort alone.

Linde and colleagues concluded rather persuasively that Hypericum is superior to placebo in the treatment of mild to moderate depression and that it has a very benign side-effect profile. Evidence is less persuasive when it comes to comparing the relative efficacy of St John's Wort with other anti-depressants, mostly because adequate studies have not been performed. Studies comparing herbal and synthetic anti-depressants used dosages of the synthetic compounds that were lower than those often used in clinical practice.

Clearly there is room for more research on the efficacy of St John's Wort, especially into questions of who would best benefit from Hypericum versus conventional anti-depressants, how best to regulate dosage and how to blend Hypericum with conventional anti-depressants. To date, there have been no head-to-head comparisons between St John's Wort and the SSRIs. Such a comparison is part of the design of the multi-centre US study currently being planned under the aegis of the US National Institute of Mental Health. It is important to compare these two types of anti-depressant, since the SSRIs are the most commonly used anti-depressants at present and, in practice, both doctor and patient may often wish to choose between these and St John's Wort in deciding how to initiate the treatment of a depression. There have also been no long-term studies of the anti-depressant effects of St John's Wort but, in this regard, the herbal anti-depressant is no different from many of the conventional anti-depressants for which long-term studies are lacking. While these questions have yet to be resolved to the satisfaction of scientists, for the person seeking relief from the painful symptoms of depression they are of much less importance than the fundamental question, 'Does the herbal anti-depressant work?' In my view this question has already been answered with a resounding 'Yes'.

To date there has been only one study that has addressed the question of whether St John's Wort works for more serious depression. The work of Daniel in the 1930s, mentioned in Chapter 6, suggests that the herbal remedy might be helpful in severe as well as in milder cases. In recent times, Vorbach and colleagues in Germany conducted a multi-centre study of 209 severely depressed patients, of whom 38 were hospitalized at the time of the study. They used a higher dosage of Hypericum than has been used in the studies of mild to moderate depressions (1,800 mg as opposed to 900 mg) and compared this with imipramine, an old standard anti-depressant. While the anti-depressant effects of these two treatments were very similar, far fewer side-effects were reported by those receiving Hypericum than by those receiving imipramine (23 per cent versus 41 per cent). This study suggests that there may indeed be a role for Hypericum in the treatment of severe depression, though more studies in such patients are clearly needed before St John's Wort can be used with any confidence as a first-line treatment in those suffering from profound depressions.

As I have noted elsewhere, there is one study that suggests that Hypericum may be of value in seasonal affective disorder (SAD), though no one has properly researched how best to combine the herbal remedy with light therapy.

I should mention that most of the research on the St John's Wort and depression has been conducted with the Kira™ brand of the herb. This preparation is extracted from the leaves and flowers of the plant by a special method and it is unclear whether the research findings with this type of extract can be generalized to other preparations.

Side-effects of Hypericum

One of the most comprehensive surveys of the side-effects of Hypericum was performed by Woelk and colleagues in Germany. These researchers monitored 3,250 patients who were receiving Hypericum from 663 private practitioners. The vast majority of these patients were considered to be mildly or moderately depressed. Interestingly, in this survey only 30 per cent of patients were considered to have improved as a result of their treatment, approximately half the percentage of respondents reported in the far more reliable data base of the *BMJ* meta-analysis mentioned above. This might have been due to the lower dosages of Hypericum used in the general population as opposed to the 900 mg per day used in most of the controlled studies.

Of all the patients monitored, only 2.4 per cent reported side-effects and only 1.5 per cent stopped their treatment because of side-effects. The most common side-effects reported were gastro-intestinal irritations, allergic reactions and restlessness, each occurring with a frequency of less than 1 per cent. These figures were again far lower than those in the *British Medical Journal* report, where 20 per cent of patients on Hypericum in one set of studies and 4 per cent of patients in another set complained of side-effects while being treated with Hypericum.

One special side-effect concern that has been raised in regard to St John's Wort is whether it increases the sensitivity of the skin to sunlight in a potentially harmful way. As I have mentioned, the toxic or even fatal sun-sensitive skin reactions in cattle has drawn attention to the plant for decades. Could such reactions occur in humans as well? Apparently not to a troublesome degree in dosages that are ordinarily used, according to Brockmöller and colleagues in Germany, who have tested the effects of simulated sunlight in volunteers. They gave one set of study subjects four times the ordinary dosage of Hypericum in a single dose, and another set of subjects 600 mg per day for two weeks. They found only very slight increases in the tendency of the skin to tan under both conditions, and no evidence of any toxic reactions. What this means is that if you are on St John's Wort you need to be a bit more careful about exposure to sunlight as you may redden or tan a bit more easily than usual. Such side-effects are common, incidentally, with many other anti-depressants and non-psychiatric medications as well.

How Does It Work?

Before we try to answer this question, it is important to concede up front that researchers do not know for sure how any anti-depressants work. But we have a strong suspicion that most anti-depressants work by affecting the way nerve signals are conducted from one nerve cell (neurone) to another. The brain consists of millions of neurones, which communicate with one another at synapses, points at which they are in close proximity but do not actually touch. Neural signals pass along the transmitting neurone in the form of electrical impulses until they reach the synapse, where they are converted to chemical signals that stimulate the receiving neurone, where they are once again converted into electrical signals. Normal transmission of electrical signals along neuronal pathways is necessary for the proper maintenance of all brain-regulated functions, including the control of mood, sleep, eating, thinking and other basic processes that are disrupted in depression.

The chemical transmission of the signal at the synapse involves the release of specific nerve chemical messengers or neuro-transmitters, which are housed in little pockets or vesicles in the transmitting neurone, into the synaptic cleft, where they act on specific receptors on the surface of the receiving neurone. After they have communicated their chemical messages, the neurotransmitters are taken back up into the transmitting neurone again, where they are broken down by an enzyme called monoamine oxidase or MAO. This reuptake of released neuro-transmitters is handled by special transporter proteins attached to the surface of the transmitting neurone. The transporter proteins for the neurotransmitters involved in synaptic transmission have been the focus of considerable attention, because most commonly used anti-depressants inhibit the reuptake of neuro-transmitters by these proteins, a step that is thought to be the initial action that sets in motion a cascade of effects ultimately responsible for reversing the symptoms of depression.

Different neurones use different types of neurotransmitters to conduct their messages. Those neurotransmitters that have been most intensively studied are serotonin, norepinephrine and dopamine. One of the major ways in which anti-depressants differ from one another stems from the relative potency with which they inhibit the reuptake of these different neurotransmitters. These differences affect their side-effect profiles and, probably, their therapeutic effects as well.

Older anti-depressants were rather unselective in their effects, affecting many different types of receptors. For this reason they caused several undesirable side-effects. When the newer family of anti-depressants including the enormously popular Prozac™ and Lustral™ were introduced, their major attraction was that they selectively affected serotonin reuptake without affecting other neurotransmitters to anywhere near the same degree: hence their generic name, selective serotonin reuptake inhibitors (SSRIs). Another anti-depressant commonly used in the US, bupropion or Wellbutrin™, is thought to act more selectively on dopamine and norepinephrine. Most of these studies, incidentally, have been conducted on ground-up extracts of rat brains, though the results are believed to be applicable to the intact human brain as well.

Given the central role that inhibition of the reuptake of neuro-transmitters appears to play in the action of other anti-depressants, it was logical to study whether St John's Wort might have such effects as well, and that is precisely what Walter E Müller and colleagues in Frankfurt, Germany set out to study. What they found is that an extract of St John's Wort is capable of inhibiting the reuptake of all three neurotransmitters mentioned above: serotonin, norepinephrine and dopamine. Curiously, St John's Wort appears to inhibit the reuptake of these neurotransmitters in a manner different from that encountered with other anti-depressants. These are exciting findings to a psycho-pharmacologist such as myself because they have implications both in terms of the type of anti-depressant response and the profile of side-effects one might expect to encounter when using St John's Wort.

I have often treated depressed patients with a selective serotonin reuptake inhibitor such as Prozac or Lustral and have observed only a partial response or an initial response that later fades. In such situations I have found that the addition of an anti-depressant which acts primarily on norepinephrine transmission, such as bupropion or desipramine, will nicely complement the serotonergic drug and take care of the remaining depressive symptoms. I have treated some patients with such medication combinations for years without observing any loss of effectiveness.

As far as side-effects are concerned, the newer SSRIs appear to cause the most bothersome sexual side-effects in some people, whereas the older anti-depressants, which affected both serotonin and norepinephrine systems, appear to cause fewer problems in this regard. The balanced profile of neurotransmitter reuptake inhibition observed by Müller and colleagues may explain why many people appear to experience fewer sexual side-effects on St John's Wort than they do on the SSRIs.

Another important question that Müller and his colleagues tackled was whether St John's Wort has any significant effects on inhibiting the enzyme monoamine oxidase (MAO). An earlier report had suggested that it did have such activity, though this was not corroborated in a subsequent study. As I mentioned above, MAO is responsible for breaking down neurotransmitters after they have been taken back up into the transmitting neurone at the synapse. If this enzyme is inhibited, the concentrations of these neurotransmitters would increase in the synapse, which is believed to be the way in which a group of anti-depressants, the MAO-inhibitors (or MAOIs), exert their anti-depressant effects. A major problem with these drugs, however, is that they inhibit MAO elsewhere in the body, most importantly in the bowel where the enzyme is normally responsible for detoxifying chemicals contained in ordinary foods such as yellow cheese and red wine. As a consequence, if someone on an MAO-inhibitor should eat one of these prohibited foods, a serious toxic reaction can result, with marked and sometimes dangerous elevation of blood pressure. In addition, there is a potential for dangerous interactions between MAO-inhibitors and other drugs, such as the SSRIs. If St John's Wort were indeed an MAO-inhibitor of any potency, this would seriously limit its usefulness. The good news is that Müller and colleagues found that St John's Wort is *not* an MAO-inhibitor to any significant degree, which means that there are no food restrictions for anyone on the herbal anti-depressant and no concern on this basis about combining it with most other anti-depressants, such as the SSRIs. Just as with other anti-depressants, however, you should *not* take St John's Wort if you are also taking an MAO-inhibitor.

One aspect of the mode of action of anti-depressants that needs to be explained is why it generally takes anti-depressants, including St John's Wort, several weeks to have their effects. The effects on reuptake of neurotransmitters seen following administration of most anti-depressants are immediate and are therefore unlikely to be a complete explanation of clinical effects that take weeks to unfold. Current thinking is that the effects of anti-depressants on the reuptake of neurotransmitters may be just the first in a cascade of biochemical steps necessary for reversing the symptoms of depression. Certain brain changes following the administration of anti-depressants have been found to occur a few weeks after treatment is started, after a time lag very similar to that required for the anti-depressants' clinical effects to kick in. Researchers have suggested that these other brain changes may play a role in the mode of action of anti-depressants. Interestingly, Müller and colleagues have found that delayed brain changes similar to those seen with other anti-depressant treatments also occur in rats a few weeks after they have been given St John's Wort. This is another piece of biochemical evidence linking the effects of the herbal anti-depressant to those of conventional synthetic ones. It is not only in ground-up extracts of rat brains that St John's Wort has been found to resemble other anti-depressants, but also in live rat models of depression, where the herbal anti-depressant increases an animal's resistance to a variety of stresses just as is seen with its synthetic counterparts.

Research Still to Be Done

In addition to continuing the lines of research already begun and summarized above, other important research directions should be explored. I will mention a few of these.

Effects in other Psychiatric Conditions

Anti-depressants, such as the earlier tricyclics and the selective serotonin reup-take inhibitors, have been found to help individuals with psychiatric conditions other than depression. This includes panic disorder, bulimia, anorexia, obsessive-compulsive disorder and social phobia. It would be logical to explore the potential value of St John's Wort in these conditions as well as in depression. In an earlier chapter I have reported cases of panic disorder and compulsive hair pulling (trichotillomania) which appear to have benefited greatly from the herbal anti-depressant. In addition, I have described how people who have taken St John's Wort for depression have reported a decrease in their shyness and a greater ease in being assertive and initiating social contacts after starting the herb. All of these anecdotal observations bode well for the beneficial effects of the herb in these conditions. Since no formal studies of St John's Wort in these conditions have been undertaken, the herbal remedy should not be recommended as a first-line condition for their treatment. Nevertheless, St John's Wort may be considered as an option in treating these conditions where standard treatment options appear undesirable or problematic for any reason.

Wound Healing/Anti-viral Effects

Reports on the beneficial effects of St John's Wort on the healing of wounds go back almost 2,000 years and predate its use as an anti-depressant. Nevertheless, in modern times research into this particular application of the herb has lagged behind its psychiatric indications and awaits proper study. There are suggestions that extracts of St John's Wort may have beneficial effects in those infected with viruses such as HIV and herpes. Clinical trials are currently underway in the US to determine the efficacy of this herb for these conditions. There are other treatments, however, with proven efficacy against such viral infections and they should certainly be used ahead of an experimental treatment. Given the tendency for viruses to develop resistances against a variety of medications, however, the possibility of a new weapon derived from Nature's arsenal to fight these deadly killers is an exciting prospect that awaits further exploration.

Pharmacological Effects

Clearly our understanding of how St John's Wort exerts its beneficial effects and how it influences relevant biological systems is in its early phases. We do not even know for sure which of the many biologically-active compounds in St John's Wort extracts are responsible for its anti-depressant actions. Researchers suspect that the substances *hypericin* and *pseudohypericin*, formerly supposed to be the most active ingredients in this regard, may not be responsible at all. Instead attention has turned to another substance, *hyperforin*, as the one most likely to be the active anti-depressant ingredient. It would be very useful to know what the active ingredients are so that they can be distilled into a more potent or specific essence. It would also be very advantageous to know how St John's Wort is metabolized and how it may influence the metabolism of other medications which a patient may require along with an anti-depressant. Such information is lacking at this time, and although no conspicuous interactions with other drugs have emerged to date, more specific data in this area would be very welcome.

In summary, we have strong evidence that St John's Wort works well for a wide variety of depressed patients and that it is very well tolerated. As is the nature of science, each new piece of information raises new questions. For the researcher these are important questions to ask and to answer, but for the person suffering from depression who stands to benefit right now from the herbal anti-depressant, many of these questions are of secondary importance to the observation that the herb works for a diversity of problems in many, many people.

Politics and Economics
of St John's Wort

ST JOHN'S WORT

As I have mentioned, in Germany St John's Wort vastly outsells Prozac, which is the number-one selling prescription drug in the US. In recent years German doctors have written about seven prescriptions for St John's Wort for every Prozac prescription – and this does not take into account the millions of St John's Wort tablets sold over the counter. There is every reason to believe that St John's Wort can become as popular an anti-depressant in Britain and the US as it is in Germany, and if that occurs the sales of the herbal anti-depressant will take over a major fraction of the anti-depressant market. The over-the-counter availability of St John's Wort gives the herb the additional market advantage of easier accessibility as compared with prescription anti-depressants. Many patients may seek to treat their own depressions as opposed to seeking help from the medical establishment. Whatever the wisdom of such a decision on the part of the patient, this change in behaviour will mean more money in the pockets of producers of herbal compounds, owners of health food shops and, most important, patients themselves.

Private insurance companies and even the NHS are in a position to influence the relative cost of St John's Wort versus conventional anti-depressants. Should private insurers choose to reimburse patients for synthetic anti-depressants but not for St John's Wort, they would make the herbal anti-depressant more expensive than synthetic ones for some patients. The current situation in Germany is that St John's Wort is reimbursed by insurers if it is prescribed by a doctor but not if it is purchased over the counter. This seems like a reasonable guideline to follow in other countries as well.

The questions raised in this chapter, such as 'Should people be encouraged to treat their own depressions?' or 'Should active anti-depressants be available over the counter?' are worth debating in their own right and will no doubt be discussed in the years to come. Given the economic and political stakes involved in these issues, however, it is important for the consumer to be aware of the potential biases of those who are most likely to be engaged in the debate even though these biases do not invalidate the content of their arguments. With this in mind, let us examine some of the controversies that have been raised in relation to St John's Wort.

Awaiting Further Research

Should we reserve judgement about the effectiveness of St John's Wort pending the conclusion of the latest studies?

There does not seem to be much merit in this argument. In the use of St John's Wort to treat depression, the Europeans have been leaders for over 350 years. Since the publication of Commission E in Germany in the mid-1980s, St John's Wort has been actively studied there. A high-strength preparation of Hypericum was developed in Germany and when it was tested at a dosage of 900 mg per day was found to be superior to placebo in multiple controlled studies. While each of these studies may be flawed or limited in one way or another, taken together they portray a convincing picture of an active anti-depressant. While a large US multi-centre study, such as the one currently being planned under the aegis of the National Institute of Mental Health, is likely to add valuable new information to our current knowledge, it is not in my opinion a necessary step in proving the anti-depressant efficacy of the herb. In addition, if we wait several years until the results of the US multi-centre study have been analysed and presented, many depressed people who might stand to benefit from the herbal anti-depressant in the meanwhile will suffer unnecessarily. Many people have already voted with their feet and decided to go ahead and try St John's Wort. I believe they are justified in doing so.

A Serious Illness That Requires a Doctor

Depression can certainly be an extremely serious and, in some cases, even a fatal condition. But the symptoms of depression range in severity from severe cases to milder instances of feeling stressed and overwhelmed or lacking in energy and enthusiasm. In this regard, depression is like many medical problems, for example headaches, which can range from tension headaches to the intense throbbing pain of migraine or the pressure headaches that may signal the presence of a brain tumour. While tension headaches can be treated simply with painkillers, the more severe headaches need the help of a neurologist. Just as you might not consider going to a doctor if you suffered from mild tension headaches, so you might not feel the need to get medical help for mild symptoms of depression or stress.

Regardless of what one believes the ideal course of action in dealing with depression to be, a simple inspection of the numbers will indicate that it is impossible for all people with depressive symptoms to be taken care of by doctors. According to one estimate, 17.6 million people in the US alone suffer from major depression. There are approximately 38,000 psychiatrists and 17,000 GPs in the US. If all the depressed people were evenly divided among these providers, that would mean approximately 320 depressed patients for each doctor. Such numbers would pose an overwhelming case load for a practitioner, who would also be expected to care for patients with other types of disorders as well. In addition, patients with major depression constitute only a fraction of individuals with depressive symptoms. According to one widely respected population study, more than one in five adults complained of depressive symptoms in the month before they were surveyed. Many of these were regarded as suffering from what is known as subsyndromal depression, a less marked form of the condition but one that is nevertheless responsible for considerable misery and suffering. Clearly it is unrealistic to imagine that all of these people could be properly taken care of by the mainstream medical establishment and the evidence bears this out.

In a recent consensus statement in the authoritative *Journal of the American Medical Association*, a group of leading researchers pointedly observed:

> In the Epidemiological Catchment Area study, a nationwide community survey of psychiatric illness that was conducted around 1980, approximately one third of people suffering from a major depressive disorder sought no treatment for it. Of those who sought treatment, few received adequate treatment. In fact, only about

one in 10 of those suffering from depression received adequate treatment.

R Hirschfeld and Colleagues

Journal of the American Medical Association, **1997**

These same authors reviewed the psychiatric histories of people who entered various depression research studies even more recently than the 1980 study mentioned above, during the years when the SSRIs became very popular. Even so, the researchers concluded:

> The lack of any prior anti-depressant treatment of patients is striking, ranging from 67 per cent to 48 per cent, who despite being ill for a median of ... 20 years never received any anti-depressant medication. The range of patients who received adequate treatment is also sobering: from a low of 5 per cent to a high of 27 per cent.

Experts in public health have pondered the reasons why people have not received treatment for their depressive symptoms. In some cases, medical personnel may fail to make the correct diagnosis or to treat the problem adequately. In other instances, the depressed person may not recognize the problem, may be embarrassed to seek help for it, may feel afraid of going to a psychiatrist or deterred by the stigma associated with the diagnosis.

Whatever the reasons for the failure of mainstream medicine to take adequate care of depression in a large proportion of affected individuals, there is general agreement that depression is common, exacts a serious toll on the lives of those who suffer from it, is underdiagnosed and undertreated, and that there is a great deal of room for improvement in the situation.

Where Does St John's Wort Fit?

John Naisbett in his best-selling book *Megatrends* observed that one of the major megatrends in recent times is the shift from institutional care to self-care. People want to feel more empowered in terms of taking care of themselves and this is apparent in all sorts of ways. The public is becoming increasingly aware of the importance of taking certain steps to safeguard their own health, such as adhering to certain diets, avoiding tobacco and wearing seatbelts. The public use of dietary supplements such as vitamins and minerals goes well beyond the recommendations of mainstream medicine. According to a recent article in the *New York Times*, an estimated 100 million Americans are spending approximately $6.5 billion a year on vitamin and mineral supplements, an increase from $3 billion in 1990. The proliferation of self-help groups for addictions, obesity and specific psychiatric disorders is another example of patients taking their health into their own hands.

The frustration of having to deal with managed care organizations, multiple subspecialists who deal with different parts of the body, high-tech medical procedures and the sometimes depersonalized atmosphere of modern medicine have combined to alienate many patients from seeking help from doctors. In contrast, the idea of natural treatments, dispensed by a friendly health food shopkeeper and administered by oneself often seems very appealing, as Shirley's story *(see below)* illustrates. St John's Wort has therefore already found a market, particularly given the data in support of its effectiveness and benign side-effect profile. I predict this trend will continue.

Shirley: Economic Considerations

A 50-year-old American woman writes to me as follows:

> I first heard about St John's Wort as a treatment for depression when I was reading about natural remedies for menopausal symptoms. I began taking 300 mg but did not find it all that helpful. This past summer my husband suggested I up the dosage to 600 mg and that was the magic amount for the summer. Now that we have turned the clocks back again [at the onset of autumn] I am taking an additional 300 mg in the afternoon, which helps.
>
> I have been in and out of therapy since I was 25. Therapy with the right therapist(s) is helpful, but it is also expensive and time-consuming. My employer has a cap on the number of hours of therapy a person can undergo, and I am getting closer to that cap every week. I am hoping that this next calendar year is my last year of needing therapy. I was not in therapy for several long periods of my life. Often, a tragedy such as a death in the family or major surgery would send me back in.
>
> I prefer natural herbs to drugs wherever I can. I have refused to take Prozac or Lustral. I really don't want to rely on a drug to control my mood.

Whether or not one agrees with Shirley's opinions about psychotherapy, herbal remedies or anti-depressant medications, she does seem to embody the trend that Naisbitt mentions in his book. I do believe that she speaks for a very large number of people who are concerned about the cost of mental health care, interested in natural remedies and eager to take their lives into their own hands as much as possible. St John's Wort provides a solution to all of these concerns. Relatively inexpensive, highly effective, safe and mild in terms of side-effects, it offers millions of people the opportunity to help themselves.

It is, of course, critical to know when self-care has reached its limit and when to seek the help of an expert. Shirley appears to be able to make this distinction. It is an important caveat for others to bear in mind as well.

A Costly Problem, A Profitable Business

A recent study reported the annual cost of depression in the US to be approximately $43 billion a year. This amount includes the cost of treating the condition and the loss of productivity and positive contribution to the economy resulting from the illness. Even without taking into account the human suffering involved in the condition, depression is considered to be one of the ten costliest conditions to any nation's economy.

While depression is costly, its treatment is lucrative. Thus, the anti-depressants such as Prozac and Lustral are among the best-selling medications, representing billions in revenue for their manufacturers. While these medications can literally be life-savers, those who offer these commodities have a marked vested interest in maintaining their share of the market. They might be understandably concerned by the advent of an effective, off-prescription alternative treatment for depression. While some concerns about this new way of treating depression are warranted, others may be suspect, motivated by an attempt to protect economic turf.

In all cases, arguments against the self-administration of St John's Wort need to be considered on their merits. For example, a leading psychiatrist was quoted in a recent article in the *Washington Post* on St John's Wort as saying, 'If a drug has enough activity to actually treat something that is real and substantial, then it ought to be administered under somebody's supervision.' If you consider the many active drugs available without prescription, which are routinely self-administered to treat real and substantial problems, such as aspirin for arthritis or antihistamines for allergies, it is clear that this argument is not universally applied in other areas of medicine. Nor, in my opinion, does it necessarily apply in psychiatry either. Perhaps the psychiatric establishment has yet to get used to the novelty of an over-the-counter treatment for depression.

In summary, herbal treatments are here to stay. Given the demand for these substances, there is popular support for keeping such herbal extracts and dietary supplements available for general purchase without prescription. The World Health Organization released guidelines in 1992, suggesting how developing countries may incorporate herbal medications into mainstream medicine. According to pharmacologist Jerry Cott, 'the essence of these guidelines is that the historical use of a substance is a valid form of safety and efficacy information, in the absence of scientific documentation to the contrary.'

Those who practise mainstream medicine would do well to become acquainted with alternative medical approaches for which reasonable evidence of efficacy exists. Pharmaceutical houses might also profit by embracing the trend and putting their enormous resources towards helping to develop these herbal extracts. Researchers who study herbal remedies will surely be repaid for their efforts, given the effectiveness of these substances and the enormous public interest in them. Ultimately, though, the biggest winners will be those millions of depressed patients who stand to benefit from Nature's own pharmacopeia. It would be a great shame if politics and economic interests were allowed to stand in the way of their recovery.

The Herbal Way
to Feeling Good:
A Practical Guide

PART THREE

Using St John's Wort

My goal in this chapter is to provide a key to the chapters that follow and an overview of how to set about using St John's Wort. This chapter is intended as a guide to developing a strategy for the treatment of depressive symptoms with the herbal remedy.

Those considering the use of St John's Wort fall into one of two categories. Either they are not currently being treated with anti-depressants or they are. I deal with each of these situations separately.

Starting St John's Wort for the First Time

Are you mildly blue, stressed-out and down in the dumps or actually clinically depressed?	(See overleaf and the next chapter to help you to decide)
Should you consider consulting a doctor?	(See pages 156–65 to help you to decide)
How should you start on St John's Wort?	(See overleaf)
How can you monitor your progress on St John's Wort?	(See below)
Brainstorming and troubleshooting any problems	(See below and pages 197–230)

Are you:

1. stressed or feeling mildly blue, down in the dumps or under the weather?
2. suffering from moderately severe clinical depression, also known as major depressive disorder or dysthymia?
3. somewhere in between (1) and (2) above?
4. severely depressed?

Depression is not an all-or-nothing phenomenon like pregnancy, but exists in a whole range of different degrees across a spectrum that goes from feeling slightly blue to being suicidally melancholic. Clearly the degree of urgency and the appropriate steps to take in addressing the condition vary greatly depending on its severity. I will try to give you some pointers to help you choose which category best fits you or someone you care about, but clearly it is a judgement call and it is wise to err on the side of caution.

Stressed or Mildly Blue

An old advertisement for an over-the-counter cold medication observed that you can't take every cold to a doctor, and proceeded to plug the medicine in question. The advert was right. It is not sensible to go to the doctor with every cold – or, for that matter, whenever you feel blue, down in the dumps or lacking in energy and pep. On the other hand, a case of pneumonia should always be taken to a doctor – and promptly – and that applies to serious depression as well. And just as we have guidelines to help us distinguish between a cold and pneumonia, so we can distinguish between serious depression and feeling mildly out of sorts. In the mildly blue, stressed-out, under-the-weather category, I would put those whose symptoms are not seriously interfering with their work, personal relationships or other aspects of their functioning. Also, the problem should not have been going on for too long, not more, say, than for a couple of months.

If you think you qualify for this very mild category, I suggest that you read about the symptoms of depression anyway because depressed people are often not very good at recognizing how depressed they are – and they are not alone in this regard. Statistics indicate that even doctors fail to recognize and treat depression properly in a very high proportion of cases. If professionals underestimate depression to this extent, lay people can surely be forgiven for doing the same. Because many of the symptoms of depression do not actually involve sadness or depressed mood, but rather physical symptoms, they are easily attributed to other conditions. In addition, depressed people often believe that their problems are due exclusively to influences from the outside world rather than some internal problem. This set of beliefs may be associated with a fear of acknowledging that 'there may be something wrong with me' and a pessimism about being able to correct the problem. In fact, the opposite is often true as it may be easier to correct problems that stem from within yourself than those that arise in the outside world, over which you may have very little control.

If, after reflection, you still feel that you are not clinically depressed, but simply overstressed or mildly down in the dumps, you may well benefit from a trial of St John's Wort as described below. It is always important, of course, to address any underlying causes of your unhappiness in addition to taking the herbal remedy. You may also benefit from some of the suggestions listed in the chapter called *An Anti-Depressant Lifestyle*.

Starting St John's Wort: Getting the Dose Right

Since the target dosage in most of the anti-depressant studies of mild-to-moderate depression has been 900 mg of Hypericum per day, this is a reasonable dose to aim for. The Kira™ brand of St John's Wort which, for reasons that I discuss later, is the one I recommend most highly, comes in 100 mg or 300 mg dosage, at least in the UK, which would mean taking about six 135-mg pills every day. Whenever I start an anti-depressant, I always begin with a low dose and increase the dosage somewhat gradually until the final or target dose is reached. The reason for this is that some people are very sensitive to medications and it is often not possible to predict who will be very sensitive and who will not. An average dose of an anti-depressant may be far too much for such a person to tolerate, especially when just beginning the medication. If a highly sensitive person starts right out with an 'average' dose of an anti-depressant without building up to the final target dosage, unpleasant side-effects may result and the person may be disinclined ever to try the medication again. So I would rather err on the side of moving a little too slowly. In practice, this means that I start a person on 300 mg (approximately two 135-mg pills) of Hypericum once a day for two or three days, then twice a day for two or three days, then three times a day. In older people, say over 60, I would proceed even more gradually.

If unpleasant side-effects should develop, I slow down this progression, always working within the patient's comfort zone. In other words, if you are uncomfortable with two 135-mg tablets of Hypericum per day, don't move up on the dosage until the side-effects dissipate, as they generally will. Be sure to listen to what your body is telling you. Discomfort of any sort is a signal for you to slow down. In some sensitive people, including the elderly, a final dose of less than 900 mg, such as 600 mg (4 × 135 mg), may work best.

I should note that my practice of starting slowly differs from the widespread practice in Germany of starting with 900 mg per day – approximately two Kira™ tablets three times a day. According to my German colleagues, they do not experience problems with this approach.

Be sure to take the Hypericum with meals, as this minimizes the chances of developing indigestion or abdominal discomfort which may occur in certain people on the herbal remedy.

Monitoring Your Progress on St John's Wort

How can you monitor your progress on St John's Wort? The answer to this might seem obvious. Surely the medication either works or it doesn't. What is there to monitor, you might ask. Well, it is not always so clear-cut when a problem is relatively subtle to start with or when the response is modest or partial. I always find it useful to keep an eye on what are known as the target symptoms – those presenting problems that are part of the reason why someone is seeking help in the first place. We measure whether an anti-depressant is working or not by focusing on changes in the target symptoms. In the case of someone with mild symptoms of depression or stress, such target symptoms might be lack of one's usual enjoyment or enthusiasm for life, decreased energy, anxiety or sleep difficulties. It is worth listing these target symptoms and observing each week whether you can observe any improvement in them. A log such as the one provided below can be helpful in tracking your progress.

Monitoring Effects on Target Symptoms

TARGET SYMPTOM   BASELINE AND WEEKS 1 THROUGH 6
(E.G. ANXIETY,
LOW ENERGY, ETC.)

Base Line	Week 1	Week 2	Week 3	Week 4	Week 5	Week 6
_____	____	____	____	____	____	____
_____	____	____	____	____	____	____
_____	____	____	____	____	____	____
_____	____	____	____	____	____	____
_____	____	____	____	____	____	____
_____	____	____	____	____	____	____

scale:

0	= no change	4	= completely better
1	= a little better	−1	= a little worse
2	= quite a bit better	−2	= quite a bit worse
3	= a lot better	−3	= a lot worse

I have been impressed with the highly variable time course of response to St John's Wort. Some people report feeling better within days of beginning the herbal remedy, whereas for others the response is far slower and more subtle. A proper trial takes at least five to six weeks. If you are still feeling down in the dumps or overstressed at that point, I suggest that you take some further step, such as consulting a GP or therapist. If you are feeling better and are not suffering any significant side-effects, you may wish to stay on the St John's Wort regimen for a further three months before thinking of tapering it and determining whether you can maintain the gains without any further help from the herbal remedy. If you experience unacceptable side-effects, feel free to lower the dosage and see whether you still feel better. You can always raise it again later if you need to.

Clinical Depression

Major depressive disorder and dysthymia are officially recognized conditions, as defined on page 150. By definition major depressive disorder disrupts one's capacity to function and enjoy one's life. It is reasonably severe and lasts for at least two weeks. Dysthymia is less severe in terms of the number of symptoms required for its diagnosis, but is by definition rather chronic and, as such, also exacts a toll of one's life. The criteria listed on pages 148 and 150 can help you to decide whether you might be suffering from one of these two conditions. If you are, I do recommend that you consult a doctor, but this certainly does not mean that you cannot take – or benefit from – St John's Wort. Involving a doctor in one's care can be challenging, especially when you are dealing with an 'alternative' treatment such as the use of an herbal product. To guide you as to how best to involve an appropriate doctor in helping you with your problem (or in extricating yourself from an inappropriate one), please consult Chapter 11.

The directions for getting started on St John's Wort are the same as those described above. If you experience no response within five weeks, however, and are experiencing no unacceptable side-effects, you may consider pushing up the dosage to eight, 11 or even 13 135-mg tablets per day. Maintain the three times a day dosing schedule, remembering to take St John's Wort with food, and wait at least three or four days between dosage increments. There is a range of effective dosages for all other anti-depressants and there is no reason to believe that such a range would not apply for St John's Wort as well. Sometimes a full clinical response to an anti-depressant will not be observed until the dosage is pushed into the higher levels of the accepted therapeutic range. So far there has been only one published clinical trial in which 1,800 mg (about 13 Kira™ tablets) of St John's Wort were given per day. According to the researcher in charge of the study, levels of side-effects were not noticeably higher for the 1,800-mg per day dosage than he has generally observed when treating people with the more conventional 900-mg per day dosage.

Unless the depression is really severe, it is quite reasonable to use St John's Wort as a first-line treatment, in combination with other methods of promoting an anti-depressant lifestyle, as outlined in Chapter 12. Monitor your symptoms as described above. In addition, those suffering from major depression may find the more extensive log on page 234 a helpful guide for monitoring your level of depression. Since it is a daily log, as opposed to the weekly log provided above, it enables you to get a more fine-tuned sense of your mood control and helps you to recognize influences that may have an adverse or beneficial effect on your mood. Subtle mood cycles can also become apparent, and their pattern may suggest certain specific types of treatment.

Once again, allow five to six weeks for the treatment to work. If it doesn't work by that time, consult your doctor about either adding an anti-depressant or switching to a more conventional anti-depressant. On the other hand, if you have detected a partial response and your symptoms are not too severe, you may want to wait a further few weeks before deciding on making any other medical changes.

Between Mild and Major Depression

Technically, those who don't quite meet diagnoses of major depressive disorder or dysthymia are known as *subsyndromal*. Studies on subsyndromal conditions have found that they can actually be quite disabling, often causing as much misery and costing those suffering from them as many days off work as the full-blown syndromes themselves. Clearly this is a mid-zone, where judgement is required as to whether to involve a doctor or not. It's not a cold, it's not pneumonia, it's more like bronchitis or laryngitis, something nasty but not deadly. Seeking out medical attention is certainly the prudent course in such situations, but in reality, people often choose to take matters into their own hands. Whether or not you choose to involve a doctor in the treatment of your symptoms, St John's Wort can certainly be used, often to good effect. Follow the same guidelines for dosing and monitoring as outlined above.

Severe Depression

If your depression is severe, I recommend that you start treatment with a conventional anti-depressant as opposed to St John's Wort.

I would regard depression as being severe if it disrupts important functions, such as personal relationships or work to a major degree, if it is seriously interfering with physical functions such as sleeping or eating, or if it is accompanied by a sense of hopelessness or suicidal ideas or plans. To date, there has been only one study with St John's Wort for relatively severe depression. Although the results of that study revealed a beneficial effect of St John's Wort equivalent to a modest dose of a conventional anti-depressant, there are numerous studies indicating the value of more conventional anti-depressants in severe depression. At this point the benefits of St John's Wort for severe depression must be considered somewhat experimental, and a more proven first-line approach makes more sense, given how much is at stake when depressive symptoms are severe. Severe depression can jeopardize a person's job, relationship or the successful outcome of a project. Of even greater concern is the danger of suicide, which is a major risk of severe depression. A delay resulting from starting with a less well-established approach is therefore too risky. A doctor should be consulted and a trial of a conventional anti-depressant should be initiated without delay.

If you are already on one or more anti-depressants or mood-regulating drugs and are considering either switching to St John's Wort or adding it to your current regimen, it is worth asking yourself these questions:

Is your current regimen controlling your depressive symptoms with an acceptably low level of side-effects, are you still depressed (at least in part) or are you bothered by unacceptable side-effects? Why, when and how should you involve your doctor in your decision to switch to or add St John's Wort?	(See overleaf and Chapter 11 for more information)
How should you go about switching to St John's Wort or adding it to your current regimen?	(See overleaf)
How can you monitor your progress on the new regimen?	(See above)
Brainstorming and troubleshooting any problems	(See below and Chapter 13 for frequently asked questions)

If you are currently being treated with one or more anti-depressants and are considering using St John's Wort, you need to ask how to proceed if:

1   You are doing well, your depressive symptoms are under good control and side-effects are at an acceptably low level.

2   You are already being treated for depression but are not doing as well as you would like either because your depressive symptoms are not under control or because side-effects are unacceptable or undesirable.

When Depressive Symptoms Are Under Control

I recommend that you stick with your existing programme. If your depression is well controlled and the side-effects of your current treatment regimen are acceptable, you have reason to be thankful. Not everyone attains such a good resolution to the problem of depression. Don't switch to St John's Wort just because it is a herbal remedy or an exciting form of treatment. It might be less beneficial than what you are already taking and you might experience a relapse of your symptoms. It is more important to feel better than to be fashionable. So don't mess with success; enjoy your good health.

When Depressive Symptoms Are Not Under Control

If your depression has been treated with only partial success and side-effects of your current treatment are unacceptable, it may be worth adding St John's Wort to your current treatment regimen provided you are not being treated with a type of anti-depressant called an MAOI. Brand names of MAOI anti-depressants are Nardil and Parnate; if you are taking them your doctor should have warned you not to eat cheese or drink red wine while on these medications. Apart from the MAOIs, it appears that St John's Wort can be combined with all other anti-depressants quite safely.

Be sure to consult your doctor before adding St John's Wort to what you are already taking. Even though it is a herbal remedy, it is an active anti-depressant and can interact with the medications your doctor has already prescribed. That is, after all, the very reason for adding it in the first place. As such, it cannot be considered in the same category as adding vitamin C to your existing medications, which would not necessitate a call to your doctor.

SUGGESTED DOSING SCHEDULE

Since you are already taking anti-depressants, it is wise to start St John's Wort more slowly than if there were no other anti-depressant in the picture. Start with two 135 mg tablets for at least a week, before adding two more and then waiting a second week before adding another two (to make a total of six). You may once again need to wait several weeks (at least four) before being able to judge with any degree of confidence whether the addition of the herb has made a difference to your mood. In some cases, however, evidence of mood improvement can be detected much sooner. Side-effects may also develop more readily, and I have encountered jitteriness, for example, in some patients who add St John's Wort to an anti-depressant, especially one with activating qualities of its own. As always, slowly incorporating the herb into your current medication mix is the best way to safeguard against developing unacceptable adverse effects.

If you are currently being treated with conventional anti-depressants and are experiencing unacceptable side-effects, you will need to reduce the dosage of anti-depressants that you are currently taking before getting relief from these side-effects. In other words, simply adding St John's Wort is not going to remove the side-effects caused by another anti-depressant. After decreasing the dose of the other medication, you can then add St John's Wort in the hope that it will have the beneficial effects of the drug that is being tapered, without its adverse effects. I usually recommend overlapping the two drugs and moving slowly in reducing the dosage of the old one while increasing the dosage of the new one. This strategy is often used in switching from one anti-depressant to another and tends to minimize the unpleasant feelings that may be associated with the medication shifts. Once again, listen to what your body is telling you as it is often the best guide as to how to pace the medication changes. All the same reasons for involving your doctor in this change of medications apply here as much as in the previous example or, possibly, more so. When you reduce an anti-depressant that has been working, you risk suffering a relapse and may really need your doctor's help and support in getting the medication adjustment right and helping you get through the transition period.

In summary, if you are considering starting St John's Wort to treat depressive symptoms, develop a game plan, which should involve all of the following elements: (1) Decide where your symptoms fit in on the depressive spectrum, which can range from mild to very severe; (2) Decide whether it makes sense to involve a doctor in your treatment; (3) If you decide to take St John's Wort, review the guidelines for how to start treatment, adjust dosage and monitor your response. While all of these elements have been discussed to some degree in this chapter in order to provide you with an overall approach to treatment, much more detail is provided in the chapters that follow, which should answer many, if not all, of the questions you may have about St John's Wort and how best to use it.

Diagnosing Your Own Depression

People often confuse clinical depression with sadness. That's a mistake. You can be sad without being clinically depressed, and vice versa. Let's say, for example, that you have been rejected by a person you love, have been made redundant or have suffered some major setback in some project in which you have invested a lot of time and energy. It would be strange not to experience some feelings of sadness in the days or even weeks following such a reversal of fortune. But if such normal sadness is short-lived and not accompanied by some of the tell-tale signs of depression listed below, no doctor would diagnose you as being clinically depressed. You would expect to see the feelings of sadness diminish over days or weeks and be replaced by other feelings – elements of relief, hopefulness or even happiness and, together with those feelings, optimistic thoughts. Maybe it wasn't such a great relationship and you're better off out of it. And the job wasn't necessarily that terrific, now that you think of it; some other job may suit you better. And as for the reversal of fortune, it hurt, no question about it, but it wasn't critical. You take your knocks, learn your lessons and move on.

As you will see in the pages of this book, a capacity to get on with things is not a hallmark of depression. When you are depressed, you feel trapped and stuck. Solutions do not present themselves to you. It can seem as though there is no way out. So sadness by itself does not mean you are depressed, even though sadness is certainly one of the cardinal symptoms of depression. Often this is not an ordinary sadness, focused on a single situation or event. Rather it is a pervasive sadness that seems to settle on everything. The sadness can take over all other feelings, leaving little room for happiness, contentment, good humour or even anger. But even though sadness is one of the most common symptoms of depression, it is also one of the easiest to connect with the condition. In our everyday language, a person might say 'I feel sad' or 'I feel depressed' interchangeably. In contrast, there are other symptoms that may be less obviously associated with depression, but are nevertheless cardinal symptoms and signs of the condition. I have called them the seven tell-tale signs of depression. It is easy to attribute these signs, incorrectly, to conditions other than depression. But when they are present, depression is one condition that should always be considered.

The Seven Tell-Tale Signs of Depression

1   Running on empty
2   Nothing seems like fun anymore; life seems dreary
3   Putting yourself down
4   Failure – at work and in relationships
5   Biological disturbances: sleeping, eating, weight and sex drive
6   The future looks bleak
7   Life seems not worth living

Running on Empty

Not long ago the newspapers reported that the president of Harvard University was unable to return to work. Amid speculations as to what might be wrong with him, his doctor issued a bulletin saying that he was exhausted from overwork. He was 'running on empty'. Well, you don't have to be the president of Harvard University to know how that feels. I have encountered this symptom in depressed patients I have treated from all walks of life. I recall a highly skilled psychotherapist who was in such great demand because of his expertise that he received many more referrals than he could comfortably handle. Unfortunately he was much more skilful at taking care of his patients than of himself, and had a hard time isappointing his referral sources. He seriously overbooked his schedule, leaving much too little time for rest, exercise and recreation. As a result, his depression was extremely difficult to treat. No matter what anti-depressants I gave him, he always seemed to be running on empty.

Population studies suggest that depression is becoming more common with each successive generation, our youngest people being most frequently affected. No one knows why this should be happening. One possible reason is that it is a cost of upward mobility. As we become an increasingly sophisticated technological society, the newly created opportunities carry with them certain risks and hazards. Increasingly, there are businesses that stay open until all hours of the night. People take their computers on holiday with them so that they can plug into their e-mail and connect to the Internet from the most remote places. They carry cellular phones and are always on-call, wired in and connected to their business associates and customers. And businesses themselves, in an attempt to become more competitive, squeeze the most they can out of each employee. One patient of mine, a chemist who supervised several pharmacies, kept being given more and more shops to supervise. Just as with the psychotherapist I mentioned, her depression was very hard to treat and only responded, finally and completely, when she quit her job.

The curious thing about depression, though, is that you can end up running on empty regardless of how great your burdens are in any objective sense. Each of us has our comfort zone in which we can function happily and efficiently, and each has our limit beyond which our capacity to function breaks down. When someone becomes depressed, that breaking point has been exceeded. It does no good to debate whether or not you *should* be able to handle the level of stress. Regardless of the objective level of stress that you are currently under, if your capacity for handling that stress has been exceeded, you will feel as though you are running on empty and that may be an indication that you are clinically depressed, especially when it is combined with some of the other tell-tale signs of depression.

One of the hardest things to do when you are running on empty is to start new projects. New initiatives invariably require a new burst of energy, which is especially difficult to muster when you are down.

It is also important to remember that running on empty may be a symptom of other illnesses. Chronic infections, such as glandular fever, may strip you of energy, as may many other medical disorders. Chronic fatigue syndrome (CFS; also known as ME) is a particularly vexing condition, in which low energy level is the cardinal and sometimes the only symptom. Low thyroid function and other hormonal conditions may also result in fatigue and low energy levels. These can generally be diagnosed by simple blood tests. This is one reason why, in the best of all possible worlds, you should get a medical evaluation before reaching a definitive diagnosis of depression. Or, if you don't choose to do that, to re-evaluate the situation if you try to treat your depression and it hasn't improved substantially within a month or two.

If you have been running on empty for more than a few weeks, consider the possibility that you may be clinically depressed.

Nothing Seems Like Fun Anymore

Life is difficult. This is how M Scott Peck begins *The Road Less Travelled*, one of the most successful books of all time. As he points out, this statement is one of the great, inescapable truths, which has been emphasized by philosophers since the time of Buddha. Hard work, losses, injustices, illness and poverty are among the problems that are part of our human condition. Despite these difficulties, however, the capacity of the human spirit to rise above such difficulties time and again has repeatedly been observed. Victor Frankl survived one of the greatest horrors of our modern era or, perhaps, of all time – the Holocaust – and went on to write his classic inspirational work, *Man's Search for Meaning* in which he emphasized our capacity to find significance and value even in the most horrible of circumstances. He regarded such an ability to preserve a sense of purpose and meaning as essential to survival.

Depressed people lose their capacity to see meaning and significance in their lives. A religious person when depressed may feel cut off from God, a particularly distressing loss at a time when spiritual comfort may be most deeply needed. In such a spiritual void, the depressed person may naturally feel that there is very little purpose in living.

Related to our ability to find a sense of meaning and purpose in life is our capacity to enjoy ourselves and have fun. We can see this ability at play even in the midst of all sorts of difficulties. Poor people retain their ability to celebrate, as anyone can see who has walked through the impoverished neighbourhoods of some European town during the festival for a saint or at carnival time. Even very hard-working people take time out for recreation. When difficult times let up, even for a short interval, the ability to have fun pops up again like the crocuses that sprout their shoots and flowers after a long winter.

All of these normal abilities are the opposite of what we see in depression. Even in the midst of plenty — enough money, good physical health, supportive friends and family — the depressed person is unable to have a good time. This inability to enjoy life can come on insidiously and it may take a while to realize that you are not enjoying life as you used to. Sometimes this recognition is triggered by returning to a place you've been before or an activity you used to relish and realizing that you don't have the same feelings or enthusiasm for it that you enjoyed before. Sometimes friends will ask you what the matter is. You just don't seem to be enjoying yourself as you used to. Suddenly or gradually you realize that nothing feels like fun anymore. As one of my patients put it, depression is like an unwelcome guest that follows you around your house and just won't go away. The formal clinical term for this state is *anhedonia*, which means the inability to experience pleasure. Life feels dreary. Sometimes this dreariness is experienced through the senses. Colours seem less bright than they did before. The world may look grey or dark where formerly it was full of vivid colours. Whatever it is that you may have loved – music, dancing, films – now feels like a drag. In this way, depression is like a thief that robs you of the joy of living. This is another reason not to delay in treating it and reclaiming the ability to experience joy once again.

If nothing seems like fun anymore and life seems dreary, and this has been going on for more than a few weeks, consider the possibility that you may be clinically depressed.

Putting Yourself Down

Self-criticism is part of the way we regulate the quality of our performance in the various aspects of our lives – our work, our relationships and even our pastimes. We are constantly judging ourselves. This often begins first thing in the morning when we look in the mirror. How do I look today? Are there bags under my eyes? Is my hair OK? Do these clothes fit properly? Do they suit me? Or when we step on the bathroom scales. Have I gained a pound or two? Did I overeat last night? Or drink too much? Either the question is answered or the answer is deferred. And so it goes on, for most people, throughout the day.

At the office, you might ask: How did I handle that last meeting? Did I say the right thing in the right way? How did it go over with the boss, the client, the organization? Was the product up to my usual standard? A parent may ask, 'Is my child doing OK and, if not, am I to blame?' A homemaker may ask, 'Am I keeping up with the housework or taking care of the home properly?' In our relationships we may ask, 'Am I a good enough wife, husband or lover?' or 'Am I getting the love or attention I want and need?' And so it goes. We ask, we judge, we reach conclusions. This is an important ongoing process because it is a feedback loop by which we calibrate the quality of our lives and the basis for making changes or corrections so that our needs are met and we feel good about ourselves and the way things are going.

In depression, though, this whole process is disturbed. We see ourselves through a distorting lens. In the extreme case, the depressed person feels ugly and a failure in all areas that matter. Such judgements are made more confusing by the fact that the disorder itself causes us to fail in many ways, as I describe below. Even so, it is typical of a depressed person to exaggerate these failures far beyond what is reasonable and accurate. And it is this tendency to extreme exaggeration that is the major tell-tale sign. The conclusions reached by a depressed person, far from being an accurate take on reality, are in fact yet another manifestation of this multifaceted disorder. 'I am a terrible housewife, nothing I ever do turns out right,' or 'I'm a terrible mother; my children would be better off without me,' are common laments. 'I'm no good at all at what I do, I deserve to be given the sack.' The distortions may be projected into the future, as in 'I'll never amount to anything,' and 'I have fooled people into believing I'm competent and sooner or later I'll be found out.' Sometimes the distortions are so gross that they would almost seem comical were it not for the pain and distress of the person experiencing them. For example, one colleague quotes a patient of his as saying, 'I am the most unimportant person in the world.'

Whenever you find yourself using exaggerated phraseology in connection with yourself, such as 'the most,' 'the worst' or 'the least,' you should suspect yourself of being the victim of distorted perceptions and very possibly suffering from depression. Such distortions have been a focus of one of the most successful forms of psychotherapy for depression, namely cognitive therapy, in which the distortions are systematically challenged and subjected to scrutiny, using the patient's capacity to reason, which is often intact in depression. Cognitive therapists have actually shown that such rigorous challenging of aberrant perceptions and ideas can correct not only the distorted thinking of the depressed person but can also result in a beneficial effect on the person's mood.

If you are in the habit of putting yourself down or constantly seeing yourself in the worst possible light and this has been going on for more than a few weeks, consider the possibility that you may be clinically depressed.

Failure

Depression cuts into a person's ability to function so that some of the failure that they perceive does have a basis in reality. Mental processes slow down and it is difficult to concentrate, to focus or to get things done. Work inevitably suffers; chores remain undone; things get botched up, leaving you with feelings of failure and inadequacy, many of which may be exaggerated but some of which may be true. It is easy to forget how competent you have been at other times and how much you have accomplished before. All these things seem insignificant when you are depressed. Dr Kay Redfield Jamison, in her wonderful memoir

An Unquiet Mind, describes the difficulties in thinking she experienced during one of her depressions as follows:

> Everything — every thought, word, movement — was an effort. Everything that once was sparkling now was flat. I seemed to myself to be dull, boring, inadequate, thick brained, unlit, unresponsive, chill skinned, bloodless, and sparrow drab. I doubted, completely, my ability to do anything well. It seemed as though my mind had slowed down and burned out to the point of being virtually useless. The wretched, convoluted, and pathetically confused mass of gray worked only well enough to torment me with a litany of my inadequacies and shortcomings in character, and to taunt me with the total, the desperate, hopelessness of it all.

This description of severe depression conveys many aspects of a depressed person's thinking. In the years that followed the depression described above, Dr Jamison went on to succeed enormously as a psychologist, researcher and writer, but such a future is unthinkable when you are in the depths of a depression. It is important to realize how misleading the conclusions reached in a state of depression can be. Nevertheless, when you are depressed, the difficulty in thinking and functioning is real and has its consequences. Failure that occurs in the context of some of the symptoms of depression described here should therefore be considered a tell-tale sign of depression in its own right.

Failure occurs in the workplace, but also in personal dealings. Relationships require a capacity to attend to another person and an ability to feel engaged with that person, both of which are sorely impaired in depression. Others may well feel put off, and withdraw in response to the reclusiveness of a depressed person.

If you find you have been failing at work or in your personal relationships in a way that has not always been typical for you, and this has been going on for more than a few weeks, consider the possibility that you may be clinically depressed.

Biological Disturbances

One major difference between sadness and depression is that the latter is often accompanied by changes in biological functioning. These biological changes are among the most reliable tell-tale signs of depression, and when doctors and therapists look for depression they carefully inquire about changes in sleeping, eating, weight and sex drive. You should certainly pay special attention to these important behavioural functions in evaluating whether you are depressed and, if so, how severely depressed you are.

In depression, sleep is often disrupted. Some depressed people have trouble falling asleep; others toss and turn or wake during the night; and early morning waking, often with difficulty returning to sleep, is very common. Sleep doesn't seem to have its usual renewing properties and people are often left feeling tired during the day and desperate at night for sleep that stubbornly refuses to arrive. Some depressed patients sleep too much, at times for hours each day more than is normal for them and yet, once again, find that no matter how much they sleep, they still don't end up feeling refreshed.

These two patterns of sleep disruption – insomnia and oversleeping – may signal two distinct types of depression, one representing a state of hypervigilant overarousal and the other a state of torpid underarousal. These patterns may reflect exaggerations of different types of response to stress.

When people (or animals, for that matter) are stressed, a part of the brain known as the hypothalamus activates a stress-response system, which results in release of certain hormones from the adrenal glands, particularly cortisol. In addition, the fight-and-flight part of the nervous system, known as the sympathetic nervous system, is activated. These changes result in arousal and vigilance, qualities that are necessary for combating stress, and are associated with decreases in sleep and appetite. The type of depression associated with decreased sleep and appetite and weight loss may represent an exaggeration of these arousal responses. Evidence to support this theory is found in the form of elevated cortisol levels in the circulation and other signs of overactivity of the stress-responsive hormonal system in these depressed patients.

The heightened arousal and vigilance that are part of our normal response to stress should be time-limited in order to be most effective. Ideally, such responses should kick in following a stressful situation, such as the loss of a loved one, a physical challenge or an important deadline, and taper off when the stress has been successfully handled or resolved. In depression, the stress response may be triggered either by a definable stress or by some unknown factor, but whatever its original trigger it then takes on a life of its own, persisting long after the stress is over. Consider, for example, a person susceptible to depression who is told that he has lost a large sum of money on the stockmarket, whereupon he plummets into a deep depression. If that same person is told a week later that his stockbroker has made a mistake and that he has actually made a lot of money instead of losing it, will his depression immediately disappear? Probably not. Such is the nature of depression that once it gets going, it can continue indefinitely. As you can imagine, this wears the system out and the person is left feeling exhausted and depleted.

The second type of depression – the one associated with oversleeping, overeating and weight gain – may represent an exaggeration of the energy-conserving responses seen frequently in animals. The hibernating bear, for example, goes into a state of low activity and torpor designed to conserve its energy and resources. Such shutting down of bodily activities enables the bear to make it through a winter of severe weather and scarce food. Most people with seasonal affective disorder (SAD), many of whom compare themselves to hibernating bears, experience this second type of depression and tend to oversleep, as well as overeat and gain weight, during their winter depressions.

Withdrawal and seclusion often occur in animals as a response to stress or injury as part of the recovery process. An injured lion, for example, will retreat to its lair until its wounds have healed before venturing back out into the savannahs and exposing itself to the dangers of the wild. An infant monkey separated from its mother initially goes into a state where it cries out pitifully, which was termed the stage of protest by John Bowlby, a pioneer in the area of separation and loss. Later the infant goes into another state that Bowlby called detachment, where it withdraws from contact with other animals. It has been suggested that these stages are ways by which the animal adapts to the loss of its mother. Initially, it makes noises, which would have the function of attracting the attention of the mother, who might not be far away. After a while, however, if the mother has not responded, the infant goes into a state of withdrawal at this point and waits until another parental figure might chance to come along. In the course of evolution, it has probably proven far more adaptive for the infant not to carry on crying, which might attract a predator, and instead to go into this detached state. There is a final stage that has been described in such separated infant monkeys – a stage of reattachment, whereby the infant will reattach to such a new parental figure that might arrive on the scene. Over the millennia, certain adaptive behavioural changes to injury and loss have evolved so as to maximize the chance of survival. It has been suggested that some of the behavioural and physical symptoms of depression may represent disturbances of the normal biological systems responsible for mediating such adaptive responses.

When an animal is stressed, the emphasis is on survival, as well it should be. Having sex is the last thing that will be on that animal's mind. And so it is that with the depressed person, the sex drive diminishes and may shut off completely. Every aspect of sexual functioning may be affected – arousal, enjoyment of sex and the capacity to function. Needless to say, this does not much help the self-esteem of the depressed person, which is already at a very low ebb.

So we see that in depression there may be an exaggeration of some of our very useful responses to the stresses and challenges that life deals us. When these responses – such as hypervigilance or excessive withdrawal – go too far, they hinder rather than help our ability to adapt. They continue for much too long and we are unable to turn them off by an act of will.

If your sleeping, eating, weight control and interest in sex are disturbed and this has been going on for more than a few weeks, consider the possibility that you may be suffering from depression.

The Future Looks Bleak

Just as depression tends to cast a grey pall over everything in your world and in yourself, so there is an irresistible tendency to project that gloomy view into the future. The depressed person will always find something to be pessimistic about. And as with one's view of the present, these gloomy predictions are often without any reasonable basis in reality. And even when there are problems in a person's life, there are many different ways to look at one's future. A person with cancer, for example, may have a very optimistic and upbeat view of the future, whereas a depressed person in perfectly good physical condition may be full of gloomy predictions about his health. In fact, in one research study patients who had suffered from both cancer and depression were asked to rate which of their two conditions involved greater suffering. They rated depression as the more painful of the two conditions. In summary, there is not generally a very close correlation between the realistic prospects for a person's future and how a depressed person is likely to view it. Pessimism is a cardinal symptom of depression.

If the future seems bleak and gloomy to you and this has been going on for more than a few weeks, consider the possibility that you may be depressed.

Life Seems Not Worth Living

As you can imagine, with all the symptoms I have just listed, including a grim and bleak view of your present situation and future prospects, a depressed person may easily reach the conclusion – or entertain the possibility – that life is not worth living. This symptom of depression, known to the clinician as suicidal ideation, is a very troublesome one. If you are experiencing any such ideas, please do yourself and everyone who cares about you a great favour and consult a doctor without delay. Depression is a condition where hope is in short supply and one way to get an infusion of hope is to reach out to those who may be able to guide you out of the dark place. Your doctor is a logical first port of call in such an attempt to reach out. But if, for any reason, it is difficult for you to talk to your doctor about the problem, tell someone – a family member, friend, or even someone on a crisis hot line. Suicidal ideation is not a symptom that anyone ought to have to suffer alone.

As depression deepens, suicidal ideation may progress to passive suicidal longings, which may be accompanied by lack of self-care or carelessness. A depressed woman may feel a lump in her breast while taking a shower and may say to herself, 'So what if it's cancer? It would probably be all for the best anyway.' Another depressed person might cross the road carelessly and, in the back of his mind, be thinking, 'Well, if I get run over, what loss will that be to anyone?'

Matters become even more serious when suicidal ideas begin to gel into actual plans, and even more so when actions are taken to put these plans into effect. It might seem unnecessary to say that if someone you know or love should mention suicidal ideas or plans to you, these should always be taken seriously.

Unfortunately it is still all too common for people to minimize the seriousness of such communications. The idea that if someone tells you he is considering suicide, he is unlikely to act on it, is a very dangerous myth. Such divulgences should always be heard as a communication of despair, which may or may not involve immediate danger but which always warrants serious attention. At the very least it is an expression of severe mental anguish.

If you think that life is not worth living or have any thoughts or plans to end your life, you are very, very likely to be depressed. Please don't delay in getting professional help for this problem.

The Clinical Diagnosis of Depression

The diagnosis of depression has always been – and continues to be – made largely on the basis of a person's subjective history. Although a skilful clinician will see traces of depression in a person's face, observe sluggishness or agitation in the body's movements and hear the slow cadence in the voice, it is the depressed person's own story that will carry the day in making the diagnosis. A few decades ago there was great optimism that a laboratory test for depression could readily be found. No such luck. For better or worse, in your recollections of how you have been feeling and your accurate take on your present mood you hold the key to determining whether or not you are depressed. What the skilled clinician does is to organize these recollections and evaluate whether or not they meet modern diagnostic criteria for depression.

I remember well, before modern systems of diagnosis had been developed, how the question of diagnosis would be debated in teaching hospitals. A patient would be interviewed and there would be discussion to and fro as to the exact diagnosis. Finally the professor would opine as to whether he (and yes, it was almost always a man) thought that the patient was depressed or not. And his opinion would prevail because he was the boss. Well, clearly that was a most unsatisfactory state of affairs. For clinical, research and, more recently, insurance purposes, it became necessary to define depression.

The latest diagnostic classification system is called DSM-IV, a handbook referred to by insurance companies and others to determine a person's clinical diagnosis. Each diagnosis is given a specific code number. The diagnosis for many psychiatric conditions, including clinical depression (referred to officially as major depressive disorder), was reached by the so-called Chinese menu approach. In Chinese restaurants, the fixed-price menus permit you to have a certain number of items from Column A, a certain number from Column B and so on. That's how it is with the DSM-IV criteria for major depressive disorder, which I have modified and listed below. It is worth checking whether you meet the criteria for major depressive disorder. It is important to remember that these are strict criteria. If you do not meet these criteria, that does not mean that you are not depressed and might not still benefit from St John's Wort and the other remedies mentioned in this book.

DSM-IV Criteria for Major Depressive Disorder

A Five (or more) of the following symptoms have been present for two solid weeks. This is different from your usual functioning. At least one of the symptoms must be either (1) depressed mood or (2) loss of interest or pleasure.

1 depressed mood most of the day, nearly every day, either experienced by yourself or observed by others

2 markedly diminished interest or pleasure in all, or almost all, activities, most of the day, nearly every day

3 significant weight loss when not dieting, or weight gain, or decrease or increase in appetite nearly every day

4 sleeping too much or too little nearly every day

5 being agitated or depressed to such a degree that others could notice it – not just internal feelings of restlessness or being slowed down

6 fatigue or loss of energy nearly every day

7 feelings of worthlessness or excessive or inappropriate guilt nearly every day – more than just feeling guilty because your depression doesn't enable you to function adequately

8 decreased ability to think or concentrate, or difficulty making decisions, nearly every day

9 recurrent thoughts of death (not just fear of dying), recurrent ideas of suicide or attempting or planning suicide

And

B These symptoms cause significant distress or impairment in your social, occupational or other important areas of functioning.

And

C The symptoms are not directly due to the physical effects of medications, drugs or alcohol, nor the result of a medical condition, such as underactive thyroid functioning.

Now, many people who feel quite depressed do not exactly fit into the DSM-IV criteria for major depression. The diagnostic schema allows for these types of depression as well. These include briefer depressions that occur premenstrually (*premenstrual dysphoric disorder*), milder depressions (*minor depressive disorder*), and recurrent depressions that can be very severe even though they may last for only a few days at a time (*recurrent brief depressive disorder*). The good news is that all of these depressions, as well as those that accompany medical conditions or may be associated with drugs and alcohol, may be helped by the same treatments that are helpful for major depression.

One diagnosis, which has its own code in DSM-IV, is *dysthymic disorder*, a milder form of depression that causes a great deal of misery because of its chronic nature. I have modified the DSM-IV criteria for dysthymic disorder and have listed these below.

DSM-IV Criteria for Dysthymic Disorder

A depressed mood for most of the day, for more days than not, either experienced by yourself or observed by others, for at least two years

And

B presence, while depressed, of two or more of the following:

1 poor appetite or overeating
2 insomnia or sleeping too much
3 fatigue or low energy
4 low self-esteem

5   poor concentration or difficulty making decisions

6   feelings of hopelessness

And

C   during the two-year period, you have never been without the symptoms in A or B for more than two months at a time

And

D   the symptoms are not due to the direct physical effects of medications, drugs or alcohol or to a general medical condition, such as
underactive thyroid functioning.

As you read through the criteria, it will become obvious that they are somewhat
arbitrary. What if you were free of symptoms for two-and-a-half months? Does
that mean that you are not dysthymic or wouldn't benefit from treatment?
Although systematic diagnostic schemas have been useful for standardizing
diagnoses for research and other purposes, the seasoned clinician and the clued-
up patient should realize that diagnosis is not a precise science and not get too
hung up on whether someone exactly meets the criteria or not before deciding on
whether and how to treat. It is clear that when we are dealing with depression
in all its forms, we are dealing with a continuum, with happy normal mood at
the one end and serious depression at the other and all sorts of gradations in
between. The same treatments that help the more severe forms of depression will
generally also help the milder forms and vice versa. The most important determi-
nants of whether or not you seek and receive treatment are therefore how bad
you feel and whether you are willing to reach out for help.

How Bad Is Your Depression?

One point that bears repeating is that depression exists on a spectrum of severity, ranging from mild feelings of low energy, sadness and being stressed out to full-blown suicidal melancholia. It is obviously very important to determine the severity of depression in order to treat it properly. This determination has relevance not only for the use of St John's Wort but as an overall guide to optimal treatment. As I have mentioned, the strongest evidence for the benefits of St John's Wort come from studies on mild to moderate depression. If depression is mild or even moderate, it may be reasonable to try a home remedy before seeking medical help, at least for a limited period of time. Severe depression, on the other hand, should be regarded as a medical emergency and treated by a doctor without delay. In such cases, it would pay to start out with one of the more conventional anti-depressants, which have a more proven track record in the treatment of severe depression.

One way to distinguish between mild-to-moderate depression versus severe depression is to examine how well you are doing in those areas of life that are important to you. How are things going in your relationships, at work and in your ability to enjoy your leisure time? If they are going badly, this might be a clue that your depression is more serious than you realize. When considering the impact of depression on a person's life, it is extremely difficult to disentangle cause and effect. A depressed person is quite likely to perceive the mood problem as being a result of all that is not going well in his or her life, when actually the reverse may be true. Are you depressed because of a bad marriage, a bad job and difficult life circumstances or are these difficulties occurring because you are depressed? Given the impossibility of answering this question with any degree of certainty, it is best to assume that the depression is the culprit that is souring the rest of your life because it's usually the easiest thing to fix. So in judging the degree of your depression, consider how things are going in the various compartments of your life.

Reading through the list of symptoms in the major depression criteria listed on page 148 will also provide you with a guide to the severity of your depression. In general, the more symptoms you have, the more severely depressed you are. Each symptom can in itself be measured according to its severity. In fact, that is how researchers measure depression – by asking about the severity of a large number of depressive symptoms, giving each symptom a score and then adding up the symptom scores to obtain a total. It is worth asking yourself how bad your various depressive symptoms are, and if you find that they are cutting into your functioning to any significant degree then it pays to consult a doctor. I will discuss this further in the next chapter.

The Monkey on Your Back

Depression has often been compared to a beast. It is a beastly condition. Winston Churchill called it his black dog, conveying how it seems to attack from outside and overwhelm us with gloom. In everyday terms, we speak of having a monkey on our back. But depression is a monkey that comes in different shapes. And it is worth considering its different shapes because this can help us to understand and treat the type of depression in question.

Depression can come as a single episode or be recurrent. When recurrent episodes consist only of depressions, the condition is called *unipolar. Bipolar disorder*, on the other hand, means that depressed episodes are interspersed with manic or hypomanic (a bit less marked than manic) episodes, when a person becomes excessively activated, overtalkative and sped up. Manias and hypomanias can cause major problems in their own right, a full discussion of which goes beyond the scope of this book. An important thing to bear in mind, however, if one has a tendency to bipolar disorder, is that all anti-depressant treatments have been shown to be capable of inducing manic or hypomanic episodes. So far there have been no reports to my knowledge of St John's Wort inducing a hypomanic episode, but as it is an active anti-depressant treatment it would come as no surprise if such complications of treatment were to be reported.

Recovery from depression may be complete. Alternatively, depressions may be superimposed on a dysthymic disorder, in which case recovery is not complete but the remission of the more serious depression may return the unfortunate individual to the chronic state of misery that is the hallmark of dysthymia. This type of depression has also been referred to as *double depression*, indicating that a really bad depression can be superimposed on a milder, more chronic underlying depression.

Depressions may take on a seasonal pattern. The most common type of seasonal pattern is marked by winter depressions, which improve in the summertime, a condition known as *seasonal affective disorder* (SAD). Some people with SAD do not recover completely in the summertime although their depressions may become much less severe. In other words, they have a type of double depression. Such a seasonal pattern is worth noting since it suggests that the winter depressions may respond favourably to light therapy. People with SAD have also been found to benefit from St John's Wort as I have described. Some people have regularly recurring seasonal depressions at times of year other than the winter, particularly the summer.

People with *recurrent brief depression* (RCB) have frequent depressive episodes that usually last between two and four days. Despite their brevity, these depressions cause a great deal of pain and studies show that about a quarter of these individuals have attempted suicide at some time in their past. I once asked a patient with this type of depression how depressed he had been on average. He replied that on average he had not been very depressed at all, but pointed out that I had asked the question in the wrong way. 'You can drown in a river that is only six inches deep on average if it has some very deep places in it.' And that is how it feels to have recurrent brief depressions. All of a sudden you can feel as though you are drowning. It is only recently that much attention has been focused on RCB even though it appears to be quite common. So far, no studies have shown much benefit from anti-depressant medications for this disorder and no studies of St John's Wort have as yet been undertaken for this condition.

At this point, you should be able to identify whether you have the symptoms of depression, how severe these symptoms are and whether they fall into some definable pattern. The next question is what to do about it. Should you consider going to a doctor? Is St John's Wort worth a try and if so, how should you go about using it? These are some of the questions I tackle in the chapters that follow.

Enlisting a Doctor's Help

ST JOHN'S WORT

In earlier chapters I have provided some guidelines as to how to diagnose your own depression and when it might make sense to involve a doctor in its treatment. In this chapter I go into greater detail about this. Essentially there are five reasons for involving a doctor in the treatment of depression. First, if depression is severe, it is risky to treat it on one's own. In addition, there is far less evidence for the efficacy of St John's Wort in severe depression than there is for more conventional anti-depressants. Second, other conditions may masquerade as depression. A visit to a doctor may uncover the real reason for symptoms and lead to a specific and effective treatment for them. Treating such conditions with conventional anti-depressant strategies may be ineffective and will delay treatment of the underlying problem. Third, there may be other psychiatric problems that are worthy of attention in their own right and depression may even be secondary to these other problems. Treating these other conditions may be the first order of business and requires the help of a doctor. Fourth, it can be difficult to be the best judge of your own mood and progress, and a skilful observer and experienced clinician is an invaluable companion in the treatment of depression. Finally, depression is a lonely condition and a good doctor is also like a good friend to cheer you on through the dark wood into a better and brighter place.

Severe Depression Needs Urgent Medical Attention

The voice on my answering machine says, 'I am calling to cancel my appointment for tomorrow. I am just too upset to come in and talk about it.' This is the paradox of severe depression. It is a downward spiral. You feel so bad you have no wish to seek assistance nor any hope that it will help. You become more isolated and depressed. Work and relationships suffer, compounding the problem, and so it goes. You can be helped but you have to get to the doctor if this is to happen. And sometimes, if you can't manage to do so yourself, a loved one or friend must take you there. Often this takes relatively little work on the friend's part, but what a difference it can make!

Someone rings me to ask me to ask to see his friend, who is very depressed and needs help immediately. I am closed to new referrals, I say, but something in the friend's voice changes my mind. If someone has a friend who cares so much for him, somehow that makes me care more too. I become involved, recruited to be a member of the team and help the friend out of his depression. Two months later the friend is completely well (on Lustral, incidentally, not St John's Wort. It was too acute and serious to warrant my trying the herbal anti-depressant, though, in future, as we learn more about the herb it may become a first-line treatment even for more serious depression).

Serious depression can cost a person his or her life. It can wreak havoc with relationships and jobs. It is a medical emergency – and it is treatable. So it is clearly a reason to seek out medical help without delay. And if you have a friend or loved one who is severely depressed, do go the extra mile or two to connect him or her with a good doctor. It is really worth the trouble and effort to do so.

Depression Masquerading as Other Conditions

Some of the symptoms of depression may be the result of a different condition. Low energy level and fatigue may be symptoms of medical conditions, such as low thyroid functioning, which can be diagnosed easily by means of a simple blood test. But there are other conditions as well that can masquerade as depression.

A neighbour of mine, a highly successful scientist and a charming person in his mid-fifties, seemed to undergo a change of personality over the course of about a year. During this time he walked around feeling fatigued and down in the dumps for many months. His sleep was restless and he would frequently wake up during the night. These symptoms might easily have been mistaken for depression. A visit to his doctor and, subsequently, to a sleep laboratory, revealed that he had a condition known as sleep apnoea. He stopped breathing for short intervals numerous times during the course of the night, which would wake him up. As a result of his breathing difficulties, his brain was not receiving sufficient oxygen. Small wonder that he was exhausted during the day, felt miserable and had difficulty concentrating. The problem was entirely corrected by a continuous positive air pressure (CPAP) machine, which ensures that he receives sufficient oxygen throughout the night. He became once more his cheerful self and I would see him tirelessly mowing his lawn and attending to his garden. We would once again chat and share jokes and his mood was completely restored with the help of one critical substance upon which all of our lives depend, namely oxygen.

This same person later developed weakness and tiredness and again lost his usual ability to concentrate and function normally. Another visit to the doctor and some simple blood tests revealed that his blood chemistry was abnormal. This turned out to be due to a rare tumour of the adrenal gland. Removal of the tumour corrected the problem and restored him once again to his previous high level of functioning.

In summary, many of the symptoms of depression are not unique to this condition, but may also be the result of medical conditions, some of which such as low thyroid levels or sleep apnoea are relatively common, while others such as tumours of the adrenal are rather rare. A visit to a competent doctor can often help sort out whether there may be a medical condition masquerading as depression. Even if you choose not to go to a doctor in the first instance but decide instead to try and treat your own depression, it is still worth bearing these other medical conditions in mind in case the symptoms do not resolve within a reasonable amount of time.

Depression Co-existing with or Secondary to Another Condition

Sometimes one type of psychiatric condition can mimic another. For example, an accountant in his mid-forties was referred to me for treatment of his low mood. He was very discouraged about his work, where he was constantly in trouble for procrastinating. He was very intelligent and had no difficulty understanding the complexities of his clients' finances but somehow he had insurmountable problems with deadlines. He would leave things until the last minute, stay up all night working crazily and would almost always succeed in getting the work done on time. But these last-minute all-nighters were becoming tiresome not only to my patient but to his associates as well. As a consequence he was under pressure to work in a more steady and even manner and he was depressed at his difficulties in doing so.

Careful questioning revealed that he had suffered from attentional difficulties since childhood, had never performed up to his potential and had always relied upon the intense pressure of deadlines and the prospects of failure to motivate himself to get anything done. In lectures and classes he would lose track of what the lecturer or teacher was saying. He was extremely distractable and often left tasks — particularly boring and unpleasant ones such as paperwork — half completed as his attention shifted to something which at that moment he found more interesting. I diagnosed him as suffering from attention deficit disorder (ADD), prescribed Ritalin, a stimulant, and recommended certain behavioural changes in the way he approached his work. He responded immediately and favourably and his mood improved as well. He turned out to be someone whose depressed mood was the result of another problem which responded to treatments that were specifically helpful for that condition. An anti-depressant alone would have been unlikely to correct his fundamental problem, namely his attentional difficulties.

Even if a person is indeed depressed, it is worth going to see a doctor to determine whether some other treatable condition may be present in addition to the depression. Shakespeare noted that 'when sorrows come, they come not as single spies but in battalions.' And so it is that depression is often accompanied by some other condition, such as a drug or alcohol problem, attention deficit disorder or an eating disorder. If these conditions are present they deserve to be treated in their own right with the appropriate treatment. People with more than one condition often require more than one type of treatment to get the best results.

Judging Your Own Moods

When you are depressed it is easy to lose your objectivity. Often it seems as though your unhappy feelings are a reasonable response to the behaviour of others, whereas it may be that others are withdrawing from you because of your depression. Similarly, a setback at work may be the result of poor concentration and ability to focus, which are well-known symptoms of depression. A good clinician will point these facts out to you and increase or modify your medications so as to control depressive symptoms that have been only partially treated. One useful way to monitor your own moods is to keep a log of them, such as the one provided on page 235. Learning to evaluate your level of depression is an acquired art and, after being in good treatment for some time, many people become extremely skilful at gauging and managing their own moods.

Doctor as Companion

In a recent article, the eminent doctor and author Sherwin Nuland writes about the deficiencies of modern medicine in which the doctor treats the disease but not the patient who is suffering from the illness. Being ill is a lonely and scary condition and, of all illnesses, depression must surely be one of the loneliest and scariest. A good doctor should be a source of comfort to you in your illness and in the recovery process. You would do well to invest the time and energy in finding a doctor who is not only technically competent but is also able to play this critical role.

Choosing a Doctor

I can't emphasize enough how important is the choice of a doctor. I am often astonished by how some highly discriminating people, who are careful in the selection of their barber or hairdresser and will go to great lengths to buy the right car at the right price, will take pot luck with whatever doctor is in their neighbourhood. I always like to go to doctors recommended to me by other doctors, figuring that if you're in the trade yourself, you know the wheat from the chaff.

Credentials are of some value in choosing a good doctor, but sometimes doctors trained at the best places can also be conceited and closed to new ideas. In seeking a doctor, find someone who is clever, up-to-date, sympathetic, open-minded and not too impressed with his or her own opinions. Find someone who will take the time to listen to you and really hear what you are saying. Finally, keep an eye on your doctor. Even the best doctors are only human, can make mistakes and don't always think of all the possibilities. Even if you are in treatment with a good doctor, you still have some responsibility to use your wits to be sure that you get the best possible care.

Extricating Yourself from an Unsuitable Doctor

A good doctor should not only keep up with the literature but also be open to learning new things. Ignorance is human and often forgivable; it is, after all, a treatable condition. Closed-mindedness, however, is hard to treat and if your doctor is not open to new information, that is a real problem since medicine is constantly changing and new diagnostic and treatment approaches are regularly being developed. It can also be very distressing to end up with a doctor who, rightly or wrongly, reflexively dismisses your point of view, as illustrated by the following cautionary tale.

Jennifer, a woman of about 40, has suffered for some years from both winter depressions and attention deficit disorder (ADD). I have treated her depressions with Prozac, accompanied by light therapy in the winter, and her ADD with Ritalin. She is an intelligent and artistic person who has used her sensitivity to light to create paintings in which bright colours sweep across large sheets of canvas, creating the impression of vivid sunsets or tropical birds flying across azure skies.

Troubled by the weight gain that she has experienced since starting Prozac, Jennifer went to see her doctor, who was listed in a local magazine as one of the best in the area. She explained to him that the weight gain appeared to be a direct result of being on Prozac. He told her that was impossible, that Prozac causes weight loss, not weight gain. She told him that I had mentioned that I had seen weight gain as a result of Prozac and related anti-depressant medications and that this often followed an initial period of weight loss. She pointed out that I had even made mention of this observation in a book of mine. He told her she must have misunderstood me and was certainly mistaken in her facts. She began to cry. He became increasingly upset with her for disagreeing with him and told her he wanted to end the appointment right there and then. She subsequently received a letter from the doctor, striking her off. Although the experience was quite traumatic for Jennifer, she is obviously better off without this doctor. The moral of the story is simple: If a doctor is unwilling to listen to you and take your comments seriously, you are better off with someone else. All of us should have our minds open to new information.

Another patient of mine did not wait for her doctor to dismiss her. She dismissed him. This woman, who was in her early twenties, had suffered from recurrent depressions for many years. She had been treated on Lustral with some success, but in order to obtain the full effect the dosage had to be increased into a range that made her feel uncomfortably 'wired'. She decreased the dosage of Lustral and wanted to add St John's Wort to the mix. She consulted her doctor, who told her that it was dangerous to do so because he had read that St John's Wort was a monoamine oxidase inhibitor (MAOI) and the two classes of drugs should not be used together. While St John's Wort had initially been thought to be an MAOI, subsequent information revealed that the herb does not inhibit the enzyme monoamine oxidase to any significant degree and that there is no good reason why it could not be administered with Lustral. The young woman searched the literature and decided to try St John's Wort on her own in conjunction with Lustral. She responded very well to the combination and experienced no side-effects whatsoever. She continued to see her doctor regularly and, after some time, plucked up the courage to tell him what she had done. He became very angry and chastised her for taking the herbal remedy behind his back. At that point she decided to change doctors. She could forgive him his ignorance about the herb and his tendency to be controlling, but it really hurt her to think that he would be more upset that she had defied him rather than happy that she was feeling better.

Sometimes it is as important to extricate yourself from an unsuitable doctor as it is to find a suitable one.

An Anti-depressant Lifestyle

Live in rooms full of light

Avoid heavy foods

Be moderate in the drinking of wine

Take massage, baths, exercise and gymnastics

Fight insomnia with gentle rocking or

the sound of running water

Change surroundings and take long journeys

Strictly avoid frightening ideas

Indulge in cheerful conversation and amusements

Listen to music

Advice to Melancholics –

A. Cornelius Celsus, 1st century AD

It is typical for us humans to expect everything to fly into our mouths without work, art, effort, grief and suffering. But all of this is not God's way; rather, it is His will that we should work hard for our food and that we should want to support both ourselves and those around us.

Paracelsus, 1493–1541

There is an old joke about a bookseller who is trying to sell a book to a student. 'It will do half your work for you,' he claims. 'Great,' says the student. 'I'll buy two copies.' It is only human for us to want to have all our work done for us or all our problems solved by a simple remedy such as a pill. The bad news – and, of course, it is not really news at all – is that wondrous though a pill may be, St John's Wort included, it will not cure all that ails you. The good news is that there are so many ways to help yourself, many of them quite painless and even pleasurable, as the advice of A. Cornelius Celsus above would suggest. Celsus was the doctor to the Emperor Tiberius, a cruel, powerful and frightening man, and the gentleness of Celsus' advice was perhaps as much politic as it was wise. Paracelsus, an outspoken man, fearless and impolitic in the conduct of his own life, had no qualms about expressing himself frankly. If you want your life to be better, you need to exert some effort to make it so. In my own dealings with depressed people I have found many ways in which modifying elements of one's life can contribute enormously to an anti-depressant lifestyle that works beautifully in conjunction with anti-depressant medications, including St John's Wort. In this chapter we will consider some of the many ways that you can help take control of your life and conquer your own depression.

Observing Your Own Moods

Just as you need to have some sense of the weather in order to know how to dress and whether to take a raincoat or an umbrella along, so you need to have a good sense of your mood in order to make the necessary adjustments to your lifestyle. Sometimes fluctuations in mood occur during a single day. A piece of bad news, a valuable object mislaid or an encounter with an unpleasant person may plunge you into a gloomy frame of mind for several hours, only to be reversed later in the day by a piece of good news, the recovery of your lost treasure or a visit with a friend. Recognizing the connection between your mood and these external events turns out to be enormously useful in making the hour-by-hour adjustments to help even out your mood across the day.

Other mood fluctuations occur over days and are less easy to recognize. For example, people may become depressed a few days after the clocks are turned back at the end of autumn, after returning from abroad or after a big party. In these three situations the deterioration in mood may be due to the hour's decrease in afternoon daylight, jet lag, or the delayed effects of alcohol respectively. One useful strategy for those who experience unexplained dips in mood is to keep a daily mood log, such as the one shown on page 235, which will help you to recognize the connection between mood fluctuations and external events. At times such logs can be crucial in convincing you that a clear pattern exists. For example, it was only after she had kept a log for several months that one of my patients was willing to concede that the alcohol she consumed on Saturday night was responsible for the dip in mood experienced two or three days later.

Finally, there are mood changes that have a longer period of duration, such as the monthly mood changes of premenstrual syndrome or the annual mood fluctuations that occur with the change of the seasons in people with SAD or the winter blues.

Mood may change with the environment – physical, climatic or human. One of my patients would feel depressed every time she went to her office. This seemed strange as she liked her colleagues and was passionate about the work itself. The clues to her depression lay in her associated symptoms – headache, dizziness, fatigue and difficulties with short-term memory. She worked in an air-tight office block full of office chemicals – printer cartridges, copiers, FAX machines and other sources of organic solvents. She was a victim of the so-called sick-building syndrome, and depression is one of the key symptoms that affect people suffering from this disorder. One patient with seasonal affective disorder experienced depression after she moved from a bright high-rise block of flats to a dim ground-floor studio. A third patient became depressed every time she visited her mother-in-law. The patient was very self-conscious about her looks and was constantly battling to lose weight. Somehow her mother-in-law always managed to direct the conversation to the patient's figure, often in the guise of a compliment. 'That dress really suits you,' she would say, 'it's just right for your shape. Where did you find it?' This would invariably make the patient self-conscious and depressed. In all of these cases, the first step in handling the problem was understanding it. An old medical adage is that you cannot treat before you diagnose. I therefore recommend that if you are of a moody disposition, become your own diagnostician, find out what is depressing you and then proceed to take remedial steps.

Taking Control of Your Life

Some of the most helpful things you can do to live an anti-depressant lifestyle involve taking control of your life wherever possible. One well-known animal model of depression, developed by Martin Seligman, is learned helplessness. In this model, rats in cages are given electrical shocks at random until, presumably realizing that there is nothing they can do to prevent these shocks, they simply give up and lie down, resigned or, perhaps, depressed. Life may feel like that to some people. At work, you may be faced with one difficult situation after another. Your boss may be constantly disgruntled or repeatedly abusive. Similarly, in marriage or a relationship it sometimes feels as though you just can't win. No matter what you do or say, you land up in trouble with your partner. These are topics of satire, but in reality are not very funny. For example, in the highly successful comedy series *Fawlty Towers*, the unfortunate innkeeper, Basil Fawlty, is always falling foul of his wife Sybil. On one occasion Sybil harangues him about his gambling. When, later in the episode, she checks on whether he has been betting on the horses again (which he has) he responds, 'No dear, that avenue of pleasure has been closed off to me.' In depression, where avenues of pleasure are already closed off to the depressed person, it is particularly important that extra sources of unhappiness be tackled or avoided.

Tackling Stress

There are many ways of tackling or managing stress, and mastering these techniques inevitably pays off by promoting an anti-depressant lifestyle. Improving interpersonal skills, for example, is one way of reducing the feeling that others are a constant source of unavoidable and uncontrollable stress. When I first began to supervise research assistants, I would observe that they often seemed harried and anxious. On one occasion, as a result of a shuffling of government personnel, a senior manager was temporarily assigned to me as a research assistant.

I delegated several tasks to him and, after the first week of working under my direction, he asked to meet with me. He explained that the number of tasks I had assigned him were more than he was able to manage competently in the course of his working hours. Would I be good enough, he asked, to indicate to him my priorities so that if he was unable to complete all the tasks by the week's end, only the least important task would remain undone. This research assistant taught me two invaluable lessons: Not only did I learn to become a better manager, to set priorities and be more realistic about what could be accomplished in the time available, but I learned how someone who is subordinate in an organization can politely set limits and manage his or her level of daily stress. If you are feeling under pressure at work, take some time to analyse the situation. Make a list of all the sources of stress and then try to figure out solutions to each of them. It is in the interest of the other parties involved to have these stresses resolved as well. Consider ways of presenting the problem to your boss, co-workers or even those working for you in such a way as to point out how it would be mutually beneficial if the stresses could be alleviated. For example, the final product might be superior, production might be more efficient, or the working environment more conducive to creativity or productivity. All of these goals can be legitimately presented as being in the interests of both workers and management.

Exactly the same principles apply in a marriage or other type of relationship, only more so. In these situations all parties involved usually have major investments at multiple, different levels. For example, in a marriage or relationship it is in both parties' interests to get along, not only because it is more pleasant to do so, but also for the sake of mutual investments in the form of children and other common goals. Once again sources of stress can be identified and communicated to your partner, and if this is done in the right way the outcome can diminish levels of stress, relieve the tension in the relationship and promote an anti-depressant lifestyle. The key is always to present the situation as a shared issue which it would benefit both individuals to solve together. Let us say, for example, that a husband comes home from work and goes straight to the fridge for a can of lager, ignoring his wife in the process. She is bound to feel neglected, angry and perhaps depressed. At this point she has a choice. She can attack her husband for his callous and brutish behaviour or she can take a more collaborative approach. Attacking him may make her feel better in the short run but is bound to make the problem worse. A collaborative approach may have a better chance of working in the long run. This could involve: (1) empathy – 'I understand that you are stressed and tired at the end of a hard day'; (2) communication of her feelings – 'I feel the same way after running after the kids all day'; (3) involving him in solving the problem – 'Can you think of some way that we can unwind together?'; and (4) demonstration of what's in it for him to do so – 'so that we can support each other at difficult times and maybe even figure out a way of having some fun in the process.' Obviously the way in which she chooses to handle the communication is likely to influence the outcome of the evening and either exacerbate or ameliorate her depression.

Part of the skill involved in such communications is picking the right time. A perceptive husband might recognize, for example, that the three days before his wife's period are not the best time to discuss the large charges they have run up on the credit card. Conversely, an insightful wife learns to discern her husband's moods and bides her time before discussing with him how she could use more help from him around the house or with the children.

It is also important to recognize that depression frequently causes stress in a relationship. This is of course an additional reason to treat the depression biologically. The partner of the depressed person often feels neglected. Feelings of depression can be contagious and there is a natural tendency to want to avoid a depressed person, which can isolate the person further and deepen the depression. There are some important pointers for the partner or family member of a depressed person to bear in mind. First, don't take the depression personally. It is not your fault. Frequently the family member feels responsible for the depressed person's mood, which makes him or her angry since at times nothing seems to cheer the depressed person up and there is a tendency for friends and family members to give up on the depressed person and withdraw. Second, it is not your responsibility to turn the depressed person's mood around. You can and should be supportive. It is particularly worth trying to help your friend or loved one get appropriate assistance. But you cannot expect to have a direct effect on the other person's mood. It is too much of a burden to place on yourself and is bound to leave you feeling resentful. Finally, don't ignore the depressed person and enhance his or her sense of isolation. Do what you can to include the person in activities in a non-demanding way. For example, a husband might suggest going out to a restaurant for dinner with his wife, who may feel cheered up by the food, the setting and the friendly attention. On the other hand, suggesting that it might cheer her up to have guests over is unlikely to have its intended beneficial effect because of the demands this will place on her to perform and be sociable, which might be the last things in the world that she feels like doing.

There is a great deal that a depressed person can do to keep his or her loved one involved even while in a depressed state. Simply acknowledging the depression and its impact can be helpful. For example, a wife is likely to respond favourably to her depressed husband if he says 'I know I have been down and not much fun lately, but I am trying to turn things around as best I can. Thanks for hanging in there with me.' The partner of a depressed person becomes starved for any positive feedback and comments such as this are generally greatly appreciated. Even if you are feeling sad and detached, as is often the case when one is depressed, it pays to make a point of expressing appreciation to your friend or loved one for gestures of kindness. It can be also useful to pinpoint specific things that your loved one can do that would make you feel better. This helps him or her to feel useful and counteracts the powerlessness typically experienced by those who surround and care about a depressed person.

So important are interpersonal skills in helping people overcome and avoid depression that an entire type of psychotherapy for depression, called Interpersonal Therapy, has been developed around these principles.

There are many types of stress other than interpersonal difficulties which may confront a depressed person and make matters worse. These include physical illness, financial difficulties and loss of a loved one. For all these different types of situations, help can be obtained from different types of experts, for example a sympathetic and competent doctor, a financial advisor or a religious or spiritual leader. A good doctor should not only provide specific help for

symptoms but also comfort and reassurance. I have seen people in serious financial difficulty who have been greatly relieved after turning their affairs over to a
debt counsellor or obtaining help and guidance from a financial planner. And
innumerable people have been comforted and supported over the centuries by
their priests, ministers or rabbis. Of course, *caveat emptor* applies whenever one
turns to any guide or authority figure for help. Ultimately you have to be the
judge as to whether a so-called expert is helping you or not. As always, stay tuned
to your mood barometer to judge the quality of assistance you are receiving.

Flight into Health

The two main ways that all animals deal with stress are fight and flight. It is
important to remember that a major way of managing stress is to leave it
behind. To quit. The term 'quitter' has a negative connotation in our culture, but
sometimes quitting is the smartest thing you can do. 'Take your job and shove it'
are the words of a country and western song. Who has not considered such an
approach at one time or another? Of course, it is generally unwise to quit one's
job impulsively or without due reflection. But there are times when, after careful
consideration, the healthiest thing to do may be to leave an unpleasant job and
find some other form of employment.

Epidemiological studies have shown that depression is increasing in frequency
in young people. One possible reason for this increase may be the escalating
stress placed on workers in modern organizations, where competition may be
greater and job security and working conditions less appealing than in earlier
decades. The modern workplace can be a very stressful and depersonalizing

place. In many organizations, people are being expected to work harder for smaller rewards and with less control over their work environment. This can be extremely demoralizing. To address some of these problems, many people have attempted to gain greater control over their working environment by quitting their jobs and working as freelancers. Although in doing so they have sometimes had to take a cut in pay, many have found that the greater control they have over their lives more than compensates for this sacrifice. They enjoy setting their own hours, choosing their work and, best of all, not having a boss and a bureaucracy to answer to. If you are feeling disempowered at work, it may be worth considering whether an alternative situation will work better for you.

I want to sound one major cautionary note, however. If you are in the midst of a bad depression it is unwise to make any major life decision until the worst of the depression is behind you. When you are depressed everything seems bad, including your job. I have encountered people who have quit their jobs in the midst of a profound depression and then regretted it later after they feel better, at which time they may come to appreciate the more positive aspects of their former work. The best approach to this problem is to treat the depression medically, for example with St John's Wort or some other anti-depressant, and after you are feeling a great deal better to consider the possibility that an unpleasant job situation may put you at risk of further depression or may hinder your complete recovery.

Just as it can be helpful to quit a bad job, so it can be healthy to leave a bad relationship. When this is a relationship of major significance, like a marriage, it is obviously worth spending a good deal of time and energy in making the decision as to whether to stay and try to work things out or to move on. Sometimes the most exciting relationships are also those that are most likely to trigger depressions. Dr Donald Klein described a condition that he called *hysteroid dysphoria* in which the affected person, usually but not invariably a woman, easily becomes enmeshed in a series of romantic relationships, each of which takes on the same pattern. Initially there is an intense feeling of falling in love, associated with enormous passion and elation. This is invariably followed by rejection or disappointment as the object of the woman's affection either rejects her or no longer appears to be a prince on a white horse after all but rather, in the eyes of the angry and disappointed lover, the horse's backside. A crashing depression ensues that is relieved only by the arrival of the next 'prince'. While medications often help with such problems, making someone less vulnerable to being swept off her feet and then dropped unceremoniously, it is obviously critical to address the underlying issue as well, which is that the affected person is looking to her lover as a means of regulating her mood and, until she learns how to stop doing so, she is destined to suffer from recurrent depressions as a consequence. Psychotherapy and social support can help in this process.

Even more valuable than getting out of toxic relationships is learning how to avoid getting into them in the first place. Often the resolution involves entering a relationship with a different type of person, someone who is perhaps less thrilling than previous partners, but who is a more dependable and ultimately a more satisfying mate.

In the days when psychoanalysis was the dominant force in psychiatry, the idea of improving your mood by leaving a problem behind was often frowned upon and referred to somewhat pejoratively as a flight into health. The idea was that you needed to work on a problem to resolve it rather than to run away from it. Of course, it often makes sense to work on problems, as I have mentioned, but let us not underestimate the value of leaving a problem behind. It is after all a basic animal instinct to run from certain threats, and a principle of environmental medicine to recognize toxic influences and avoid them. There is no reason why that same good sense should not apply to the treatment of depression as well.

Social Supports

Even more important than experts in alleviating the stresses of everyday life are our family and friends – our everyday supports. Researchers have found that even in rat models of depression, social supports play a crucial role in mediating the effects of stress on the development of depressive-type symptoms. In one model, researchers expose a more submissive rat in a cage to a more dominant one. The dominant rat will attack the submissive one and beat it into a state of submission, which the researchers have suggested is the equivalent of a depressed state. If they then place the injured rat alone in a cage, it will remain in a cowering, submissive posture. This will not occur if the rat is returned to a cage with its litter mates. The presence of these other rats appears to provide relief from the depressive symptoms, which do not persist.

Although it may be novel to consider the importance of social supports in protecting against depression in other species, its value in shoring up the human spirit should come as no surprise. In small communities all over the world there is considerable support from neighbours, friends and family in times of need. A good friend or, better still, circle of friends is one of the best non-pharmacological anti-depressants you can find. Cicero, writing about friendship about 2,000 years ago, observed that a joy is doubled and a sorrow halved when it is shared with a friend.

In our modern industrial society, however, where people move around more frequently and often live in more impersonal settings, the support of family and friends is often lacking. This is reflected in the Beatles' famous song *Eleanor Rigby*, where the group sings about all the lonely people and asks where they all belong. Eleanor Rigby, who 'picks up the rice in a church where a wedding has been', is a symbol for those of us who are detached from a group of supportive people. Where can such people find comfort and support in times of need? Others who fall into this category are those who come from dysfunctional families, which appear to be ever-increasing in prevalence. Often such people feel that they cannot turn to their families in times of need because they will not be understood and accepted for who they are. Such people can find enormous support and comfort by turning to support or recovery groups.

Support and Recovery Groups

Support groups now exist for many serious and debilitating illnesses, and depression is no exception in this regard. Such organizations provide up-to-date information and meetings to help members and their families cope with depression. A listing of available support groups that deal with depression and related disorders is provided in the Resources chapter at the end of this book.

Recovery or 12-step groups are modelled on the principles set down by Alcoholics Anonymous, which was the first such group to be developed. There are currently recovery groups for drug addicts, sex and love addicts, compulsive gamblers, overeaters and the adult children of alcoholics. There are also separate groups for the spouses, partners or family members of those who participate in these various groups. Recovery groups combine a programme consisting of working through a series of specific steps with fellowship, support and simple wisdom. In meetings people learn that they are not alone in their unhappiness. They are encouraged to talk freely and are listened to in a non-judgemental way without being challenged or confronted. There is a spirit of respect for what people have to say and the problems they are grappling with.

I have encouraged many of my patients with depressions and addictions to go to an appropriate recovery group, often with good results. At times I have managed to locate another group member who is willing to pick the newcomer up and take him or her to a meeting of the group. I have encountered considerable reluctance in my patients to go along with this suggestion and they have frequently cited concerns about confidentiality and their professional reputations. Nevertheless, all those who have followed my suggestion have found such groups to be quite valuable. It is very important in choosing a group to pick one where you feel you can identify with the other group members. Token contributions are requested of members. I often appeal to the ordinary human instinct (possibly genetically programmed) for finding a bargain, by pointing out to my patients that at 50 pence a meeting, recovery groups are the best deal in town.

Even if one is not an addict, these groups might still be helpful and, given the large number of groups available, it is usually not difficult to find one where you feel at home. One of my patients, a woman in her mid-sixties, has suffered from severe intermittent depressions for decades despite my best efforts at medicating her with multiple anti-depressants including St John's Wort. She would qualify as an adult child of an alcoholic as her mother was drunk through much of her childhood and died of cirrhosis of the liver when the patient was a young girl. She was reluctant, however, to go to a recovery group, so I shared with her some of the slogans that members of recovery groups often repeat to themselves and to others by way of encouragement.

To my surprise, this extremely sophisticated woman, a veteran of many years of all sorts of psychotherapy, repeated the slogans to herself several times and wrote them down carefully every day. The slogans I shared were:

> One day at a time.
> Just get your body there; the rest will follow.
> Fake it till you make it.

These are all useful slogans for the depressed person, who amplifies his or her troubles and projects them into the distant future. Take one day at a time, the slogan urges. If you consider all possible future problems at once they will seem overwhelming and you can drown in a sea of sorrows. In the case of an addict, this can drive a person to drink, drugs or acting out in some addictive way. In a depressive person, it can drive one to despair. In contemplating some professional or social commitment, a depressed person frequently asks, 'How can I possibly handle it?' Just get there, urges the slogan. Often your automatic pilot will take over and see you through. In a song written to encourage those in despair, the singer Billy Joel counsels the listener not to forget his second wind but rather to wait for the momentum to kick in. My patient used this way of thinking to help her get to a wedding which she had no wish to attend. Once there, however, she surprised herself by having quite a good time and afterwards felt very pleased that she had been able to come through for her friends and family. The slogan 'fake it till you make it' suggests that if you pretend you are managing, you might be surprised to discover that you really are managing after all. Things may turn out this way for all sorts of reasons. First, the anticipation of the task or event may be worse than the thing itself. In certain types of depression it is impossible to anticipate pleasure, but once placed in a pleasurable situation you may actually be capable of enjoying it. Another reason why you might make it after you fake it is related to daily or circadian rhythms of mood, whereby it is common for a person's depression to be at its worst in the morning and to improve as the day wears on.

Some people balk at recovery groups because many of the steps are geared round the concept of a Higher Power and, as such, may offend a person's religious sentiments or lack thereof. Nevertheless, the whole matter is generally handled with a light touch and in a non-coercive way that many people find acceptable.

In summary, support groups offer invaluable information and encouragement around specific illnesses including depression, while recovery groups provide fellowship, wisdom and tangible assistance for people with all manner of sorrows and problems.

Watching Your Alcohol Intake

Even if you don't have a defined problem with alcohol, it is very important for a person who suffers from depression to pay careful attention to his or her alcohol intake. First of all, alcohol is capable of interacting negatively with any drug that affects brain functioning. Even though one study of individuals taking St John's Wort suggested that the effects of alcohol on their co-ordination and ability to concentrate was no different from that seen in people on placebo, I would recommend moderation in alcohol consumption to someone on St John's Wort as I would to a person on any other type of anti-depressant. In practical terms, this generally means no more than one (or at the most two) glasses of wine or single shots of alcohol per day, depending on an individual's tolerance. As always, it is important to exercise judgement when driving or operating machinery under such combined drug influences.

Even in those who appear to handle their alcohol very well in the hours after drinking it, I have often noticed a ripple effect on mood in the days that follow. This sometimes occurs after a very small amount of alcohol (even a single glass of wine) and takes the patient quite by surprise when the association is finally recognized. As I mentioned, sometimes it is only by logging one's mood on a daily basis that a person will come to appreciate that there is indeed a cause-and-effect relationship between drinking alcohol and becoming depressed.

The Benefits of Exercise

After treating hundreds of depressed people, I have become increasingly impressed with the value of exercise as an anti-depressant. Conversely, I have often found that if a regular exerciser who is vulnerable to depression should become unable to exercise for any reason, depression frequently ensues. I know that it is a pain in the neck to be advised to exercise when you are depressed and it may be the last thing in the world that you feel like doing. But it really works.

There are by now several controlled studies indicating the benefits of exercise in depression. All studies agree that exercise is superior to no treatment at all. Two studies found that combining exercise with counselling was superior to counselling alone. This bears out my experience, that it pays to combine different forms of treatment in your efforts to overcome depression. Even exercise of low intensity can be beneficial, though some find that more vigorous aerobic sessions on a regular basis work better for them.

I am often told, 'If I were able to motivate myself to exercise, I would not be depressed and wouldn't need it in the first place.' I recommend that people do whatever it takes to make exercise workable and even pleasant. Sometimes this means finding a friend or workout buddy; sometimes it means joining in some group activity. A regular class can motivate you – if you know you have to be there for a certain time, and perhaps that friends are expecting you there, you are much more likely to take your exercise seriously and not find some wonderful excuse to miss it 'just this once'. In addition, a good instructor helps you pace yourself so as to maximize your gains while minimizing the likelihood of physical injuries.

Use your creativity in designing an exercise routine in a setting that works for you. One of my patients, for example, works out on a ski-machine alongside her husband while watching videotaped movies. A friend jogs on a trampoline while listening to a pre-recorded cassette of baroque music that has a tempo that matches her jogging speed. Dance of all kinds can be appealing because of the combination of music, aerobic exercise and companionship. But we differ from one another in taste and the key is to find what type of exercise works for you.

An important point to remember when beginning an exercise programme is not to overdo it. An excellent way to sabotage a long-term exercise programme is to injure your ankle or knee, which will put you out of commission for several weeks. This will, of course, be counter-productive and you might find yourself sympathizing with the words of Winston Churchill, who defended his lack of exercise by noting that he got enough exercise acting as pall-bearer at the funerals of friends who exercised regularly. Depressed people are often careless with their physical health. So please remember to start slowly and carefully and your exercise programme will be much more rewarding over time.

Controlling Your Mood with Sleep

There is ample evidence that the amount and timing of your sleep can have a profound effect on your mood. You can use this known relationship to your advantage. Once again, a log of your mood and sleep patterns (see page 235) may provide clues as to what this relationship might be in your case. For example, you might note that after a few late nights your depression is worse for the next several days. If so, an obvious solution will present itself to you – be sure to get to bed on time as regularly as possible. In general, regular patterns of sleeping and waking, known in the trade as 'good sleep hygiene', tend to promote more even mood control.

But the relationship between sleep and mood is not always so obvious. In the 1970s, Dr Thomas Wehr and colleagues, working from a theory that a fundamental problem in depressed people was that the timing of their sleep was too late in relation to their other body rhythms, devised an anti-depressant treatment called 'phase advance of sleep'. These researchers showed that if you move the onset and offset of sleep several hours earlier in some depressed patients, for example, to 5 p.m. and 1 a.m. respectively, a remarkable improvement in mood will result within several days. Although this finding was of theoretical interest, it was regarded as impractical largely because people were unwilling to go to sleep and wake up at such inconvenient hours. Another curious relationship between sleep and depression, discovered even earlier than the phase advance treatment, is that in a depressed patient a night of sleep deprivation is often followed by a remarkable improvement in mood on the following day. This counter-intuitive effect was discovered accidentally by a depressed German woman, who observed that her mood was much better on the day following an all-night bicycle ride. Sleep deprivation has been disappointing as a treatment for depression because its benefits are generally rather short-lived, dissipating the very next day after a night of recovery sleep.

Recently, Dr Mathias Berger and colleagues in Germany have developed an ingenious way of combining sleep deprivation and phase advance of sleep so that the combined treatment is both effective and practical. In controlled studies they have deprived depressed patients of sleep for a single night and followed this up with a regimen of phase advanced sleep for several nights afterwards. After achieving an anti-depressant response, the researchers then moved the timing of sleep progressively later, an hour per night, over the next six days until they reached the patient's accustomed times of sleep onset and waking. Remarkably, without any medications whatsoever these researchers obtained stable anti-depressant responses in a high percentage of their patients. Although I have not as yet used this new combined sleep modification therapy in my own clinical practice, I am waiting for an opportunity to do so. Once again, a valuable anti-depressant treatment is being developed in Germany and we would be well advised to pay attention to it sooner rather than later.

Rooms Full of Light

In the chapter on seasonal affective disorder (SAD) I discussed the value of light therapy for those who become depressed during the dark days, whether these occur during the winter or at other times of the year. What is less well known, however, is that there is growing evidence that light therapy may also be beneficial for patients whose depressions are *not* seasonal or specifically related to environmental light at all. These people may benefit from enhanced environmental lighting by itself or, more commonly, in conjunction with other forms of anti-depressant treatment.

Fisch and colleagues in Germany set out to investigate whether light therapy might enhance the response of depressed patients to treatment with St John's Wort. They divided 40 depressed patients, whose mood changes bore no specific relationship to the changing seasons, into two groups of 20. Both groups received standard doses of Hypericum – 900 mg per day. In addition to this, one group was exposed to bright environmental light and the other to dim environmental light for two hours each day. They found that the group exposed to bright light showed superior anti-depressant effects after two and four weeks of treatment. After six weeks, however, both groups fared equally well. They concluded that light therapy may speed up the anti-depressant response to Hypericum. Even if enhanced environmental lighting did no more than this, it would still be worth considering since the weeks before an anti-depressant kicks in may seem interminable to a person suffering from the painful symptoms of depression. It is especially difficult to keep up one's spirits and optimism during the early weeks of treatment since there is no guarantee that the medications will actually work. Signs of an early response are therefore particularly welcome.

It is possible that enhancing environmental lighting may do more than simply speed up the response to an anti-depressant – it may actually enhance the response. Although this effect has not yet been demonstrated for St John's Wort, Siegfried Kasper and colleagues in Germany studied a group of depressed patients who had failed to respond to an adequate trial of Prozac. These researchers treated half of their patients with bright light and half with dim light while keeping them on Prozac. After two weeks, the patients receiving bright light showed significantly greater improvements than those receiving dim light treatment, an advantage that increased over the following two weeks of the study.

These studies suggest that combining bright light therapy with anti-depressant medications, including St John's Wort, may be a valuable strategy for enhancing the speed and magnitude of the therapeutic response even in those depressed patients who have not suffered exclusively from winter depressions.

The known interaction between light and Hypericum has raised concerns about possible harmful effects to the eyes in people receiving light therapy while on St John's Wort. So far, the only study that has addressed this question directly is that of Kasper and colleagues, who examined the eyes of their patients after two weeks of such combination therapy and found no visual changes. A recent study by Brockmöller and colleagues in Germany, showing very little increase in skin tanning in patients on clinically relevant doses of Hypericum, is also encouraging in relation to the safety of this combination. Nevertheless, if you experience any eye irritation while on the combination, check with your doctor about it. What I recommend for my patients if they experience eye strain or irritation while receiving light therapy is that they try to decrease their exposure to bright light either by shortening the daily duration of treatment or sitting further away from the light source until their eyes feel comfortable.

Warning: If you have any history of eye problems, you should always consult an eye doctor before undertaking light therapy.

As the quote from A. Cornelius Celsus suggests, it is possible to derive benefits from enhanced environmental lighting without any formal therapy simply by brightening up the interior of your house. This can be done with more lamps, including indirect lighting bounced off lightly coloured surfaces. Bright colours, especially yellows and oranges, also seem to have a cheering effect on many light-sensitive people I have treated over the years. Finally, there is no substitute for natural lighting and a walk outdoors in the sunshine can combine the healing effects of exercise and light. This benefit was actually documented by Dr Anna Wirz-Justice and colleagues in Switzerland, who showed that as little as half an hour of walking in the morning had a markedly beneficial effect on her patients with SAD. I would wager, though, that other types of depressed patients would stand to benefit from such a daily prescription as well.

Dark Therapy

Having extolled the benefits of increasing the amount of environmental light, I hesitate to confuse matters by mentioning that for some depressed people, an opposite solution may solve the problem – that is, increasing the daily exposure to darkness. Dr Thomas Wehr at the US National Institute of Mental Health has suggested that a cause of depression in some people may be our use of artificial lighting to shorten the hours of darkness to which we are exposed each day. Certain people, he argues, may be physically unable to cope with the legacy of Thomas Edison – universal illumination of the night – and may benefit by returning the night to its natural length. By adopting this strategy for one man, a middle-aged engineer who had cycled in and out of depression for years, Wehr and colleagues enabled him to stay free of depression for many months simply by asking him to remain in darkness for 12 to 14 hours each day. Since then a few other individuals have derived similar benefit from this treatment. Although at this time extending the hours of darkness remains a highly novel treatment that may benefit only a few of those patients who cycle in and out of depression, it is another demonstration of the importance of the environment in regulating mood, and the value of manipulating the environment as part of an overall treatment plan for depression.

Avoid Frightening Ideas

In depressed people the most frightening ideas do not generally come from fear of the outside world but result from turning the darkened lens of depression towards the interior and finding it to be full of self-doubt, self-criticism, guilt, recriminations about the past and grim predictions for the future. All of these thoughts are not only symptoms of depression but, according to the cognitive theory of depression, developed by Dr Aaron Beck and others, can actually propagate the depression and make it worse. Based on this theory, these researchers have developed a psychotherapeutic approach to depression called cognitive therapy, which has actually been shown to be as effective as anti-depressant medications in some studies of mild to moderate depression.

Cognitive therapists have developed a way of breaking down depressive thinking into its different components and showing how once you recognize these specific types of depressive thoughts, you can actively work to overcome them. For example, these therapists have accurately recognized the tendency of depressed people to engage in what they refer to as 'all or none thinking'. So a depressed person may regard a project that was not a dazzling success as a total failure. Most ventures in life are not total successes or failures but some mix of the two. A positive attitude enables a person to enjoy those elements of the mix that are successful while learning from the failed elements, and then to move on to the next project. This is very hard for the depressed person, who is likely to expend valuable time and energy obsessing about, and magnifying, the failure. The depressed person has difficulty modulating responses to all sorts of stimuli.

Several other specific distortions of the depressed mind are also worth noting. One is overgeneralization. A depressed person who makes an error is quite likely to think, 'You see, nothing I ever do succeeds.' Cognitive therapy would seek to challenge this distortion by encouraging the depressed person to find areas in life where he or she has clearly succeeded. Overgeneralization is commonly seen following rejection. A depressed person is likely to take a single rejection as a sign that nobody will ever accept him or her. A healthier approach would be to accept that rejection is part of life and that a single rejection does not necessarily mean that others will follow. Excessive sensitivity to rejection can affect people at any age or stage of life, whether it be the child looking for a friend in the playground, the adolescent calling someone for a date, or the adult applying for a job or submitting a manuscript or proposal to a publisher or grant agency. Nobody enjoys being rejected, but we can develop ways of putting it into perspective and recognizing that further efforts might well be rewarded with acceptance. After being rejected a depressive person might avoid taking new initiatives for fear of further rejections, thereby greatly diminishing the likelihood of future success. Once again, the depressed person's intellect can be recruited to help understand that this type of thinking is a costly distortion that can be corrected with proper guidance and systematic efforts.

One of the most painful aspects of overgeneralization is that it gets projected into the future. 'I will never succeed,' 'No one will ever love me' or 'I will never find happiness' are common distortions of this type that greatly add to feelings of sadness and pessimism. Such distortions have been labelled 'fortune-telling' by cognitive therapists, a term that conveys the sense of assurance that a fortune-teller might offer about the future when plain sense indicates that there are too many imponderables to make such predictions with any degree of reliability. This can be pointed out by a skilful cognitive therapist repeatedly to good effect. Allied to this magical depressive tendency to fortune-telling is 'mind-reading', a process by which the depressed person thinks and talks as though he or she can read what is in another person's mind. So a depressed person might say 'She didn't want to come on a date with me because she thinks I am too dull and nerdy,' or an unsuccessful applicant may say 'He didn't accept me for the job because I'm not qualified.' The cognitive therapist will point out that other possible explanations for these outcomes abound. The girl who declined to go out on a date with you may already be committed to someone else; the prospective employer may have an inside candidate in mind for the job, and so on. Bearing in mind these alternative possible explanations empowers the rejected person, who is then more easily able to pursue other possibilities. In contrast, depressive thinking tends to paralyse the thinker, increasing his or her sense of powerlessness and reducing enthusiasm for making further efforts, which might be more successful.

In summary, it is important to recognize and address frightening thoughts, more technically known as depressive distortions. Fortunately, treatment strategies have been developed to tackle such thoughts and these work if they are implemented diligently and systematically.

Cultivate Healthy Pleasures

Many of the suggestions of A. Cornelius Celsus mentioned above are healthy pleasures – music, soothing sounds like that of running water, cheerful conversations, massage and travel. Whatever it is that is a source of pleasure should be sought out and developed by the depressed person because the essence of depression is the lack of capacity for enjoyment, also known as anhedonia. But even when a certain degree of anhedonia is present, some activities might still provide pleasure.

Pets, for example, can be a great source of comfort and delight even to depressed people. Many years ago I decided that it would be a useful exercise to put several of my depressed patients together in a group. I reasoned that they might be able to help one another cope with depression. In truth it was not a good idea. The group was suffused by a sense of communal gloom and despair. But I remember on one occasion when someone mentioned her dog or cat, there was an immediate change in atmosphere as each of the group members pulled out a picture of his or her pet – animals that until that moment I had not even known to exist. For some time they pored over one another's photos, admiring the animals and discussing their various special qualities and foibles. It was a vivid demonstration to me of the power of animals to cheer people up and how even depressed people are capable of spells of happiness if they are presented with the right stimuli.

Only you know what it is that delights you most when you are feeling well and how best to seek such activities out. Ask yourself what it is that still appeals even though you may be depressed. Is it painting watercolours, growing orchids or taking long walks in the countryside? The possibilities are limited only by the imagination. Consider the question, make a list of such sources of joy and then devise strategies for how you can bring them back into your life again.

I specify healthy pleasures because some pleasures are quite unhealthy, even if they are capable of bringing you out of depression for brief periods. Such pleasures may include alcohol and addictive drugs and compulsive behaviours, such as excessive shopping, spending, gambling or sexual activity. One of my patients, for example, would regularly go and shop for clothes that she could ill afford, did not need and in fact hardly ever wore. Her cupboards were full of expensive dresses that she had never even tried on after leaving the shop. For her, all the reward came from the act of shopping itself. There was something about the process of going to an expensive shop, trying on the garment, and having the saleslady pay attention to her and compliment her that proved irresistible. Of course, the comfort was very short-lived and the cost of the habit, both financially and in the form of marital conflict, severely exacerbated her depression. There are many different varieties of this habit and they can be very difficult to break. Addictive sexual behaviour is another costly way that some people use to medicate their depressed feelings. At times I have recommended specific recovery groups for these types of problems, with fairly good results.

And how do you tell the difference between a healthy pleasure and an unhealthy one? Usually it is fairly obvious. The one leaves you feeling good afterwards; the other leaves you feeling bad. The one feels like a wise investment that continues to yield dividends over time; the other like a foolish expenditure of time, money and energy, which ends up costing more than it's worth. And finally, the one is a source of pride that you might be pleased to share with friends and family, whereas the other is often a source of shame, cloaked in secrecy.

Get Help

One of my favourite *New Yorker* cartoons consists of two panels. In the first panel a drowning woman cries out to her sheepdog at the edge of the lake, 'Get help, Lassie, get help.' The next panel shows the obedient dog lying on an analyst's couch. Getting help does not always mean subjecting yourself to deep psychological examination. It can be quite concrete. An overwhelmed mother might find it invaluable to get more help with babysitting or housework. An overwhelmed student might need some special tutelage. Depressed people – like all who are ill – often feel overwhelmed by what they have to do but are ashamed or reluctant to reach out and ask for help. If you had backache or hepatitis, you wouldn't think twice about getting help so that your life might become more manageable. Well, depression is just as legitimate a condition, even if there are no X-rays or lab tests to demonstrate it. Part of getting better is accepting that you are suffering from a medical illness – depression. As one patient put it, 'Just understanding what is going on is half the battle.' Once you accept that fact, you will feel better about taking all the steps needed to help you feel better again, including reaching out to those who can make life easier for you.

Frequently Asked Questions

ST JOHN'S WORT

> In materia medica, the deductions of clinical experience often precede those of scientific analysis, and science sometimes comes later to inform us why we produce certain effects with medicines. Practice, based on clear scientific deductions, is, of course, the most desirable; but this we cannot always wait for. If a remedy long outlives what may be termed its fashionable existence and still maintains a reputation for definite remedial effects, it is reasonable to infer that such properties are not imaginary.
>
> **F A Burrall, 'Some Uses of the Oleum Hyperici',**
> ***New England Medical Monthly*, 1887**

These words, written over 100 years ago about the use of an extract of St John's Wort, are as relevant today as they were then. Although numerous scientific studies on the clinical and pharmacological effects of the herb have been published, there are many questions that have direct bearing on clinical practice for which we do not at this time have definitive scientific answers. Currently, a multi-centre research project funded by the US National Institute of Mental Health is underway to address some of the outstanding questions about St

John's Wort, for example how it compares in a head-to-head study with the selective serotonin reuptake inhibitors (SSRIs). In the meanwhile, however, until these questions are answered at the level of definitive science, those who are interested in using the herb want to get the best information available to answer certain questions they may have about it. Fortunately we have a wealth of clinical and anecdotal experience with St John's Wort, which has been used as a herbal remedy for centuries. In the past decade, millions of prescriptions for St John's Wort have been written in Germany and large numbers of people have purchased the herb over the counter and have taken it of their own accord. The growing popularity of St John's Wort has allowed clinicians and researchers such as myself to evaluate some of the questions that are on the minds of people considering the remedy for themselves and to come up with working solutions that have immediate practical implications. In this chapter I address some of the most commonly asked questions about St John's Wort and its use.

In answering some of the most frequently asked questions about St John's Wort I have drawn not only on the literature and my own clinical experience with the herb, but also on reports obtained through an informal survey and from interviews with some of the leading experts on the herbal anti-depressant in Europe. I have been assisted specifically by Professors Siegfried Kasper, Hans-Peter Volz and Müller-Spahn, chiefs of the departments of psychiatry in Vienna, Jena and Basel, and Dr David Wheatley, who has conducted clinical trials of the herbal anti-depressant in England.

For a description of St John's Wort, the plant, also known as *Hypericum perforatum*, I can do no better than to quote Dr O Phelps Brown, who wrote in 1885:

> This is a beautiful shrub, and is a great adornment to our meadows. It has a hard and woody root, which abides in the ground many years, shooting anew every year. The stalks run up about two feet high, spreading many branches, having deep-green, ovate, obtuse and opposite leaves, which are full of small holes, which are plainly seen when the leaf is held up to the light. At the tops of the stalks and branches stand yellow flowers of five leaves apiece with many yellow threads in the middle, which, being bruised, yield a reddish juice, like blood, after which come small round heads, wherein is contained small blackish seed, smelling like resin.

This description comes from a book called *The Complete Herbalist; or the People Their Own Physicians by the use of Nature's Remedies; describing the Great Curative Properties Found in the Herbal Kingdom*. Over 100 years ago, it seems, people were intrigued by the same possibilities that we are revisiting nowadays – of using Nature's apothecary as a source of remedies and of healing oneself instead of always seeking out the assistance of a medical practitioner.

The pores in the leaves of St John's Wort, which look like perforations and give the plant half of its botanical name (*perforatum*), are thought to contain the plant's pharmacologically active substances, as do the black spots on the petals. It is these black spots which, when rubbed, yield a reddish liquid that was used for dyeing clothes in earlier times.

HOW ARE THE ACTIVE INGREDIENTS OBTAINED FROM THE PLANT?

The active ingredients have been extracted from the plant in various ways over the ages. One folk remedy, used even in modern times, is to brew a tea out of the leaves and flowers. Alcohol in one form or another has also been used in the past. Angelo Sala originally used brandy to extract the active essence. In modern times, commercial companies still use a form of alcohol to extract the active ingredients, which they then enclose in a pill or capsule. The Kira™ brand is prepared by a special type of extraction with a different type of alcohol from that used in many other brands. For this reason, research results obtained with this brand cannot necessarily be generalized to other brands.

WHICH ARE THE ACTIVE ANTI-DEPRESSANT SUBSTANCES IN ST JOHN'S WORT?

No one knows the answer to this question at this time for sure. In the course of evolution, the plant appears to have developed the capacity to produce many compounds that have pharmacological effects in humans and animals. Some of these substances are toxic to animals and in this way might have served to protect the plant over millennia of evolution. We know, for example, that cattle that eat too much of the plant can develop harmful or even fatal skin reactions when they are subsequently exposed to sunlight. I should emphasize that these harmful doses are dozens of times greater than the doses used for treating depression, which are quite safe.

Most of the research on St John's Wort, both with depressed patients and in the laboratory, has been performed with an extract of St John's Wort called LI 160. This extract contains many active substances. Although most attention has been focused on two of these substances – hypericin and pseudohypericin – more attention is now being paid to a third substance – hyperforin – which appears to have some of the pharmacological properties thought to be responsible for the effects of the herb as a whole. In dealing with a herb containing such a complex mixture of active compounds, it is quite possible that more than one of the compounds is having a therapeutic effect and that they are acting in harmony to complement one another's actions.

DOES THE BRAND OF ST JOHN'S WORT THAT YOU USE MAKE A DIFFERENCE?

The simple answer to this question is 'yes.'

Professor H Hippius, formerly chair of psychiatry in Munich, writes:

> The 1996 German list of available drugs, the *Rote Liste*, includes 28 Hypericum preparations. Since these preparations are not chemically defined single-substances or combination preparations, but whole extracts of the St John's Wort plant, it cannot automatically be assumed that the various medicinal preparations from various manufacturers have the same composition and therefore the same therapeutic efficacy at the same dosage.

I agree with Professor Hippius. In other words, since we do not know which substances in St John's Wort are responsible for its anti-depressant effects, we cannot assume that all plant preparations are equivalent, even if the amount of hypericin, which is supposedly standardized across different preparations, is the same. I say 'supposedly' based on my experience with the use of certain generic anti-depressants. Generic anti-depressants are supposed to have the same amount and quality of the active compound in them as the original brand-name products. Yet I have often observed a relapse of depressive symptoms in patients who have previously been doing very well when they switch from a certain brand-name anti-depressant to its generic counterpart. If different brands of a synthetic compound produced under the supervision of the US Food and Drug Administration result in different clinical effects, how much more reason do we have to doubt the equivalency of different herbal products with their complex combinations of active substances and produced under much looser regulatory conditions? Consider, for example, how wines that are made from the same type of grape will vary in taste not only from one country or region to another but even from vintage to vintage. The substances in the wine that imbue it with its special bouquet and flavour will change with the soil, the amount of sunshine and the rainfall. A similar situation can be expected to apply to the composition of an extract of St John's Wort, where the variable of interest is not the flavour but rather the anti-depressant effects or the side-effects of the preparation.

Once we acknowledge that herbal preparations are likely to vary in their composition, where does that leave us in terms of choosing the best preparation? At this point there have been no actual studies comparing one type of St

John's Wort preparation to another. Yet most of the research in which the anti-depressant effects of St John's Wort have been established has been performed using the brand called Jarsin™ produced by the leading German manufacturer of the herbal remedy. This has led clinician and researcher Hans-Peter Volz of Jena in Germany to conclude that 'taken in sum, the anti-depressive action of Hypericum is only sufficiently documented for Jarsin™.'

The good news is that Jarsin™ is now available over the counter under the brand name of Kira™. It is essentially identical to the German compound and is clearly the brand of choice at this time.

Another reason to use a herbal product known to be made under carefully supervised conditions is that you can feel more confident that there are no potentially toxic contaminants in the preparations, such as have been known to occur in other food supplements. The contaminant in L-tryptophan that resulted in several fatalities in the US was a particularly dramatic case in point.

Some local brands of St John's Wort are less expensive than Kira™ and for certain individuals the cost difference may be a significant consideration. If this is the case, I would suggest at least starting with the Kira™ brand. If your depression does not respond, you can then be more confident that it is not because of the brand of the herbal remedy but for other reasons. Once your depression does respond to Kira™, if cost is a significant consideration you might then try to switch to a less expensive brand and see if you maintain the same level of anti-depressant response.

St John's Wort should be considered as a first-line treatment for:

- mild depression
- short-term stress associated with depression and anxiety
- moderate depression
- depression in those who are very sensitive to, or concerned about, side-effects
- winter depression (seasonal affective disorder or SAD)
- depression in the elderly
- dysthymia (chronic low-grade unhappiness)

St John's Wort should be considered, but probably not as a first-line treatment, for:

- depression in children and adolescents
- severe depression

St John's Wort should not be considered for:

- depression in pregnancy

As I discussed in the chapter on research on St John's Wort, the beneficial effects of the herb have been most convincingly demonstrated for mild and moderate depressions. There is one study in which it was used in more severely depressed individuals and proved as effective as a standard anti-depressant, imipramine. More research will be needed, however, before the herbal remedy can be recommended for more severe depressions.

A severely depressed man presented to me recently. He had legal actions pending against him and was in danger of being put in gaol. His business was in disarray and he was struggling to manage his day-to-day affairs. His desk was covered in papers that he was unable to muster the will or concentration to deal with. He could hardly sleep at all and it was an effort to fight his way through his exhaustion and get through each day. Yet it was critical that he be as functional as possible in order to co-operate with his solicitor in reaching the best possible deal with his creditors and the prosecutor's office. He also needed to be alert and active in keeping his business afloat and avoiding bankruptcy if at all possible. He needed my help urgently. Given the seriousness of my patient's depression, he was not someone in whom I wanted to try something that had not been fully researched for severe depression. I therefore chose a more established anti-depressant, nortriptyline, to which my patient responded well within a few weeks. Nortriptyline is one of a family of potent older anti-depressants, which may have a number of undesirable side-effects, such as dry mouth, constipation and blurred vision. These side-effects seemed like reasonable trade-offs given the seriousness of this patient's predicament. If the situation had been less urgent, however, I would have been more inclined to St John's Wort with its much lower likelihood to produce unpleasant side-effects.

As more research studies are performed on the use of St John's Wort for serious depression, clinical reasoning might change and the herbal anti-depressant might emerge as a first-line treatment even for severe depressions. In my experience, severely depressed people often end up on more than one anti-depressant, and there is no reason why St John's Wort should not be used as one of a combination of anti-depressants if more than one is required.

There is at least one study suggesting that St John's Wort might be useful in the treatment of SAD. Patients with SAD also benefit from light therapy and these treatments can be used together to good effect. St John's Wort should also be considered as a prime anti-depressant candidate for treating depression in the elderly because of its mild side-effect profile. Depression in the elderly is becoming a particularly pervasive problem, given our ageing population.

It is only relatively recently that clinicians and the public at large have become aware of how common depression is in children and adolescents. There has been a rapid increase in the prescription of anti-depressants for young patients in recent years. Because there have not as yet been any studies on the use of St John's Wort in young people, the herbal remedy should not be considered as a first-line treatment for these individuals. Nevertheless, I know of some cases where the herb has been used effectively in adolescents and have described one such case in an earlier chapter. In depressed children and adolescents, St John's Wort should be regarded as a second-line treatment, to be used if conventional anti-depressants prove unsuitable for any reason.

Treating pregnant women with medications is something always undertaken with hesitancy and only after very careful deliberation, given the possibility that any medication may affect the growth and development of the baby. Yet some pregnant women are so depressed that it seems wrong not to provide them with relief of their symptoms because of some theoretical risk to the baby. In such cases I try to use medications with the longest track record, particularly if there is a published literature on their safe use in pregnancy. No such literature exists for the use of St John's Wort in pregnant women, whereas there is some reassuring evidence that the older anti-depressants and Prozac might be relatively safe for the developing foetus. I would therefore prefer to use these drugs rather than St John's Wort for the treatment of depression in pregnancy.

CAN ST JOHN'S WORT BE USED IN THE TREATMENT OF BIPOLAR DEPRESSION, ALSO KNOWN AS MANIC DEPRESSION?

People with recurrent depressions can be divided into unipolar and bipolar categories. Those with recurrent unipolar depressions suffer only from periods of low mood, separated from one another by normal periods. In contrast, those with bipolar depression experience periods of exaggerated energy and activation as well as depressions. During their activated periods, known as manic or hypomanic (less than manic) episodes, these individuals need less sleep, think and talk more quickly and are more sped-up than normal. Sometimes they are elated but at other times quite irritable and angry, especially when they feel blocked, frustrated or thwarted by those around them, who appear to them to be moving at a snail's pace. The question here is whether a bipolar person can safely use St John's Wort during a period of depression.

Unfortunately there are as yet no published studies on the use of St John's Wort in the treatment of bipolar depressions. We do, however, know two important facts about the treatment of bipolar depression with other anti-depressants: (1) All anti-depressants that work in the treatment of unipolar depression also work for bipolar depression; and (2) All anti-depressants are capable of inducing hypomanic or manic episodes in patients with bipolar depression. Based on these observations, I would expect St John's Wort to be an effective anti-depressant in bipolar depressions. I would also caution anyone with a tendency to develop hypomanic or manic symptoms to be sure to use the herbal anti-depressant only under the close supervision of a doctor, and on no account to experiment with its use on your own. In addition, in most bipolar patients it is customary to use a mood stabilizer such as lithium carbonate or valproic acid before adding an anti-depressant, to guard against the development of a hypomanic or manic episode. For those of you who are wondering why one should be so careful to prevent the development of a hypomanic or manic episode, I should mention that they can be extremely disruptive and destructive to a person's life. Even though a mild hypomanic episode may not be harmful, when the process reaches its extremes it can cause the breakup of a marriage, the loss of a job, serious financial reversals and physical injury to the affected person.

I should emphasize that, to my knowledge, there has not been a single report to date of a manic episode induced by St John's Wort and that there is no greater reason to be concerned about the herbal remedy in this regard than about any other effective anti-depressant. Even so, it is good to be aware of the potential risk, especially if you have a history of hypomania or mania. One of my patients who has experienced recurrent depressions and mild hypomanias in the past is on a maintenance dose of lithium carbonate to stabilize his moods. When he developed a mild depression I started him on 600 mg of St John's Wort per day. A week later he rang me to say that he was feeling 'too good' and waking up in the early hours of the morning. I interpreted this as possible evidence of hypomania and suggested that he cut back to 300 mg a day, which turned out to be just the right amount for him. Once you are aware of the possibility that hypomania can develop with the use of any anti-depressant, you are forewarned and better able to deal with the symptoms should they arise.

HOW MUCH ST JOHN'S WORT SHOULD I USE?

Most studies of the anti-depressant effects of St John's Wort have used 300 mg three times per day. In my experience with using many other anti-depressants, however, I have been impressed by the wide variation in dosage required by different people. To some degree, this relates to the ability of a person's liver to break the anti-depressant down into inactive substances, which are then excreted. This ability varies tremendously from person to person. To some extent, one can get an indication of how sensitive a person is going to be to a new medication by reviewing that person's sensitivity to medications in the past. The amount of medication needed is often *not* related to the size of the person being treated and I have been impressed over the years by small women patients who have been able to tolerate enormous dosages of anti-depressants, in contrast to very large men who have been sensitive to tiny dosages.

I believe that there will be a range of optimal dosages for St John's Wort as well. A good practical way to begin treatment is to start with approximately 300 mg a day, with breakfast, for two to three days, followed by 600 mg a day (300 mg each at breakfast and lunch) for a further two to three days, followed by 900 mg a day (300 mg each at breakfast, lunch and dinner). As Kira™ is sold in the UK in 135-mg tablets, this would mean starting with two tablets per day, then increasing to four (two tablets twice a day) then six (two tablets three times a day). Then stay on this dosage for several weeks unless side-effects require reduction in dosage. The reason to begin with a low dosage is that whereas therapeutic effects often take weeks to appear, the side-effects of any anti-depressant may occur very soon after taking it. If this should happen, one is always better off having taken a small rather than a large dosage. In addition, it sometimes takes a while for your system to get used to a new medication, and gradually increasing the dosage gives your system a chance to adjust to it.

Taking medications with meals reduces the likelihood of developing gastro-intestinal side-effects such as nausea, indigestion or abdominal pains, which may occur with St John's Wort. The meal will not interfere with the effects of the treatment in any way. If you should develop side-effects after increasing the dosage to, say, four 135-mg pills a day and the side-effects are mild, try to remain on that dosage for at least a few days. Side-effects may settle down within a few days. If you increase the dosage without waiting for this to happen, it will most likely make the side-effects worse and discourage you from staying on the medication. It may turn out that the current dosage will be just right for you. Alternatively, if this dosage proves to be too low, once the side-effects diminish sufficiently you may be able to increase the dosage at a later time if you need to.

Taking a medication three times a day can be quite inconvenient. Somehow the midday dosage often gets missed out. It is generally much easier to take medications twice a day, and some people have found that a twice-daily dosage of St John's Wort (four 135-mg pills at breakfast and two at dinner) works well for them. One or two of my patients developed indigestion when they have used the herb in this way and found that taking it three times a day with meals completely resolved that side-effect. If you should happen to forget the midday dosage, however, it is preferable to double up the evening dose rather than missing one dose for the day, bringing the day's total to six 135-mg St John's Wort tablets. Because no one is sure of what the active ingredients are in St John's Wort, it is impossible at this time to say what the best dosing schedule really is; more research is required to answer this question. At this time, I recommend that you start using St John's Wort three times a day and, later on, after you have established that it works for you, it may be worth experimenting with different dosing schedules. It is possible that for some people, like the man whose wife mixed his St John's Wort in with the breakfast vitamins, a once-a-day schedule will prove to be sufficient.

Just as it is possible that some people will not need six 135-mg St John's Wort tablets per day but may respond fully to two or four tablets, so others may require more than six tablets per day. It is probably worth staying on six 135-mg tablets per day for at least five weeks before deciding to increase the dosage. In one study of more serious depression, 1,800 mg of Hypericum proved to be as effective as a conventional anti-depressant and the researcher running the study remarked that the frequency of side-effects did not appear to be greater than he had encountered on the more conventional lower dosage of 900 mg per day. It would be surprising to me if, just as with other anti-depressants, different people did not end up needing different amounts of Hypericum and I would encourage you and your doctor to experiment with different dosages up to 1,800 mg (approximately 13 135-mg tablets per day) provided you do not experience any particularly unpleasant side-effects and provided you give the lower dosage of 900 mg (six tablets) a fair trial of five to six weeks before increasing the dosage.

HOW LONG AFTER STARTING ST JOHN'S WORT SHOULD I EXPECT IT TO TAKE BEFORE I SEE AN IMPROVEMENT?

Although some people may experience relief from the symptoms of depression within days of starting St John's Wort, for others it may be as long as six weeks before there is a real sense of improvement. An informal survey of European psychiatrists who have treated hundreds of patients with St John's Wort revealed that most believe that one should wait at least three weeks after a full dose (900 mg per day) of St John's Wort has been started before judging whether it has been effective or not. In this regard, St John's Wort is similar to other anti-depressants, most of which take between two and four weeks to produce their initial anti-depressant effects. The reason for this delay in response to anti-depressants has been the focus of considerable research, but at this time no one has really come up with a satisfactory explanation for it. If you detect no benefit after three weeks, you have the choice of increasing the dosage of St John's Wort, switching to a conventional anti-depressant, or adding the anti-depressant to St John's Wort.

HOW CAN I MONITOR MY RESPONSE TO ST JOHN'S WORT?

Depression is by its very nature a discouraging condition and the response to anti-depressants in general is often not smooth and linear. Your mood can bob up and down and it may be hard to tell just where you are compared to where you were before you started treatment. In my practice I have used a very simple way to help my patients monitor their mood over time. On page 235 is a simple form that will help you to chart your mood in response to starting St John's Wort. Just as when you diet it is helpful to weigh yourself regularly so as to see the pattern of response, so it can be very helpful to chart your mood on a daily basis after you start a new type of anti-depressant treatment. And just as when you diet you can gain a pound or two on a particular day, perhaps as a result of water retention, even though you are succeeding in losing weight over the long run, so it is possible to have one or two bad days even though your mood may be better overall. Being able to refer to the chart is helpful in illustrating this over-all improvement. Alternatively, if you are not improving, you might be inclined to try and kid yourself that you are. Referring to the chart may reveal this not to be so and prompt you to shift your strategy in finding a different way out of your depression.

WATCH OUT FOR A PARTIAL RESPONSE

Let's say that you have been taking St John's Wort for several weeks and that there is no question that you are feeling better. Perhaps you can even see the difference on your mood chart. Should you be satisfied and ask no further questions? Not necessarily. This might be the time to get greedy. When I treat patients in my own practice I am very ambitious for them, by which I mean I want them to feel as well as they possibly can and I try to convey that same sense of ambition to them. If they are feeling quite good, perhaps they could do even better. The reason for this approach is that it is often difficult to know when a depression has been fully treated. Often there is such relief that the intense pain of depression – the dark, heavy, dismal, dreary sense of pessimism and despair – has lifted, that what remains seems just fine by comparison. Yet there may still be a sense of fatigue, low energy, insufficient optimism, drive or zest for life which may signal that elements of the depression remain. It is important to look for such elements because there is a good chance that further treatment, such as increasing dosage or adding another medication, might remove all vestiges of the depression. A friend of mine, also a psychiatrist, is fond of saying that you never know when you have enough until you have too much. Although he is referring to life in general, the same is often true about treating depression as fully as possible. Of course, if side-effects are already present it might not pay to increase dosage or add medications. That is where a careful cost-benefit analysis is in order, to weigh the potential value of further anti-depressant effects against the potential liability of more side-effects.

Besides using chemical or herbal anti-depressants, don't forget the array of lifestyle changes that you can make that will greatly enhance the effects of any of these medications, including St John's Wort, as I have discussed in the previous chapter.

WHAT IF I AM FEELING SUICIDAL?

Suicidal feelings are not a suitable condition for self-help remedies – no ifs, ands or buts. If you are feeling suicidal, you definitely need to reach out for the help of others, including a qualified professional. That does not mean that you cannot take or benefit from St John's Wort. It does mean that it's too risky for you to do so on your own without the careful and caring guidance of others. It has been said that suicide is a permanent solution to a temporary problem. Better solutions can always be found and I urge you to consult a good doctor who can help you to find them.

WHAT SIDE-EFFECTS MIGHT I EXPECT IN USING ST JOHN'S WORT?

The best data base on side-effects comes from a large German study in which over 3,000 patients on St John's Wort were monitored by their doctors, over 650 of whom participated in the survey. Only 48 patients (about 1.5 per cent) discontinued the medication in the study, and side-effects were reported by only 79 people (2.4 per cent). Of these side-effects, the most commonly reported problems were gastro-intestinal irritation, restlessness and allergic reactions, all of which were reported by fewer than 1 per cent of individuals. European experts whom I have interviewed about St John's Wort side-effects agree with these very low percentages. Such low side-effect frequencies are especially good news for the treatment of depression in the elderly, who are typically highly susceptible to the side-effects of all sorts of medications.

Although time will tell whether the initial observations of such low frequencies of side-effects are correct, I have been impressed in my own clinical practice by the absence of any side-effects in some people who have proven to be highly sensitive to side-effects from a wide variety of other anti-depressants. It seems likely that St John's Wort will indeed prove to have fewer side-effects than the synthetic anti-depressants currently in use.

As noted above, anyone with a history of hypomanic or manic episodes should be especially vigilant for the typical symptoms of activation after starting any anti-depressant. Sleeplessness, racing thoughts, pressured speech and euphoria or irritability are early warning signs of hypomania or mania that must be heeded. If these develop, you should stop St John's Wort immediately and consult a doctor. The loss of sleep (which is often not experienced as unpleasant but rather as an extra opportunity to get more accomplished or have more fun) is harmful in itself as it can fuel the manic process. If caught early, the symptoms of hypomania or mania can often be checked with appropriate actions; if not, however, they can escalate into mania, which can be very unpleasant and damaging.

A few of my patients have developed increased anxiety after beginning St John's Wort. Such reactions have also been reported to occur in certain individuals after starting all forms of anti-depressants. People with a history of panic attacks or extreme anxiety are especially susceptible in this regard. Yet anti-depressants have actually been given for the treatment of anxiety and panic. In order to overcome the initial anxiety response, which may occur after taking even a single dose, it is necessary to back down on the dosage. For example, in treating such sensitive patients with Prozac I have often started with as little as 1 to 2 mg of liquid Prozac per day. After the person has become used to that dosage, it is then possible to increase the dosage slowly and carefully over the ensuing weeks until a therapeutic level is reached. If you are eager to persevere with St John's Wort but happen to develop anxiety after taking 300 or 600 mg, it is possible to overcome the problem by obtaining a herbal extract in the form of an elixir. Begin by taking very low dosages of the elixir (say one-tenth of the recommended number of drops) and increase gradually at a rate that you can comfortably tolerate until you reach therapeutic levels.

Some people on St John's Wort have complained about increased sensitivity to sunlight both with regard to the skin, with more reddening occurring than usual, and the eyes. At this time there is no reason to believe that either of these side-effects is of clinical concern, but if they cause discomfort, protecting your skin with sun block or the eyes with sunglasses would be a sensible preventative measure.

SHOULD I SWITCH FROM THE ANTI-DEPRESSANT I AM TAKING TO ST JOHN'S WORT?

The answer to this question depends on how you are doing on your present medications. If the medicine is working with few or no side-effects, why switch? You are lucky to have found something that works well for you. As the old maxim goes, if it ain't broke, don't fix it. On the other hand, if the medication is not working well or is causing bothersome side-effects, you have good reason to be considering a switch to St John's Wort.

HOW DO I SWITCH FROM ANOTHER ANTI-DEPRESSANT TO ST JOHN'S WORT?

If you are already on another anti-depressant and are considering switching to St John's Wort, there are certain considerations worth bearing in mind. First of all, the other anti-depressant has presumably been prescribed by a doctor and it is wise to inform that doctor about what you would like to do. This should not be construed as asking the doctor's permission. As an adult, it is hardly necessary for you to do so. It is nevertheless not only a courtesy, but also of practical value as you might need to return to that doctor for advice or help of one sort or another if your experiment does not work out. In that case, it will be much easier to elicit the doctor's help if it does not appear as though you have been off on a frolic of your own. In addition, if the doctor is competent and knowledgeable, he or she might provide you with invaluable advice that will supplement the advice provided here and customize it to your particular needs. If the doctor is not open-minded about new treatments, you may wish to consider another doctor instead.

Second, as I have already noted, it is almost always useful when switching from one medication to another to do so gradually, tapering the one while starting the other, overlapping the two medications, which can be used in conjunction in the transition period. Exceptions to this rule are when the medication you are on is causing serious side-effects, in which case you might need to stop it abruptly, or if the two medications are not compatible with each other (about which more below). Even though anti-depressants as a group are not addictive and people do not generally experience severe withdrawal on stopping them, abruptly discontinuing them may result in unpleasant symptoms such as interrupted sleep or flu-like feelings. For some people these are worse than for others. For example, a few of my patients have developed the feeling that they are having electric shocks to their body after discontinuing the anti-depressant Seroxat. One factor worth bearing in mind in discontinuing a medication is its half-life. A drug like Prozac, for example, with a long half-life, persists in the system for many days after the drug is discontinued and is far less likely to cause symptoms on withdrawal. The drug Efexor, on the other hand, has a very short half-life, is excreted from the system in a matter of hours rather than days and is far more likely to result in symptoms following withdrawal. In general, withdrawal symptoms are more marked when one discontinues a drug with a shorter as opposed to a longer half-life. In addition to withdrawal symptoms, you risk experiencing a nasty relapse of your depressive symptoms after discontinuing an anti-depressant. In any event, it is generally best to discontinue an anti-depressant medication gradually rather than abruptly. Two anti-depressants may influence each other in ways that are sometimes predictable but often are not. For example, they may enhance each other's beneficial or adverse effects. For this reason it is often best if they are not co-administered in their full dosage strength.

Say, for example, that you are on Lustral 100 mg per day and want to switch to St John's Wort 900 mg per day. It might make sense to drop to Lustral 50 mg per day while adding 300 mg of St John's Wort per day for a period of three to four days. After that interval, if there are no ill-effects, one might add another 300 mg of St John's Wort together with the 50 mg of Lustral for a further four days. At the end of the second week, depending on how you are feeling, it might be reasonable to shift to the full 900 mg of St John's Wort and stop the Lustral altogether. You might expect some mood instability or side-effects during this transition time because levels of Lustral will be dropping in your blood as levels of St John's Wort are increasing, but these symptoms should be easily manageable. If they are not, slow down the process. As you can see, it is really best to have a good doctor to guide, accompany and befriend you through this transition process. With Prozac you might want to double the intervals noted above because Prozac has a much longer half-life than Lustral, which means it lingers in the system for longer periods of time.

Other medications might need to be handled somewhat differently depending on the half-lives of the medications and their particular properties.

Note

If you are on a monoamine oxidase inhibitor (MAOI) such as Nardil or Parnate, the type of medication where you are not allowed to eat yellow cheese or red wine, the above rules of transition do *not* apply. You need to wait a full two weeks after discontinuing the MAOI completely before starting treatment with St John's Wort.

CAN I COMBINE ST JOHN'S WORT WITH OTHER ANTI-DEPRESSANT MEDICATIONS?

As I have already mentioned, it is possible to administer St John's Wort with a variety of other anti-depressants and other medications in general. A survey of European colleagues who have treated collectively several hundred patients with St John's Wort revealed no drug interactions noted to date except for potential problematic interactions with the MAOIs as noted above. At one point it was thought that St John's Wort might itself be a MAOI and might exert its anti-depressant effects by that mechanism. If that were the case, it would be potentially dangerous to combine St John's Wort with other anti-depressants. Fortunately this does not appear to be the case to any significant degree and St John's Wort can be used freely with other anti-depressants. Furthermore, you need not worry that you will develop the extremely uncomfortable and sometimes dangerous high blood pressure reaction after eating cheese or drinking red wine, as can occur with those who are on an MAOI. *There are no dietary restrictions whatsoever when you are on St John's Wort.*

As I mentioned above, you might be best off moving more gradually with dosages if St John's Wort is used in combination with other anti-depressants or stimulants as these medications all act on the nerve cells in the brain and can enhance one another's effects. While this is one of the desired goals of the exercise, namely to induce a more powerful anti-depressant effect than would be obtained on any of the medications alone, it is also a reason to increase dosages gradually to avoid the development of exaggerated and unduly unpleasant side-effects.

WHAT ABOUT COMBINING ST JOHN'S WORT WITH ALCOHOL?

Alcohol itself often complicates the treatment of depression. Although de-pressed people often report a pleasant buzz after using alcohol, in my experi-ence they often pay for this buzz heavily in the days that follow. This delayed effect is often difficult to discern. If your mood is bad to start with and it feels worse on certain days, there are any number of good reasons to explain the mood worsening. The two or three drinks you had last night or the night before are by now a distant memory and hardly seem to be likely culprits. But careful observation in many patients has shown that once the alcohol is stopped, mood control is often much smoother and better. Now, if you enjoy having sever-al drinks of an evening I hardly expect these mild observations of mine to per-suade you to stop doing so, but it's worth thinking about it. If you're keeping the mood log I mentioned above, you might note when you drink (including the num-ber and type of drinks you have) and see whether you can detect an impact of the drinks on your mood over the ensuing days.

Quite apart from the potential problem of drinking alcohol if you happen to suffer from depression is the question of whether you can safely drink alcohol if you are on St John's Wort. The answer is that there is no known negative interaction between St John's Wort and alcohol. Even so, I always suggest that my patients go easy on the alcohol if they are on any anti-depressant (no more than one or two lagers or glasses of wine or one glass of spirits is what I usually recommend). After all, if these drugs are all working on the brain, it would be strange if they did not affect each other's actions in one way or another.

CAN I TAKE ST JOHN'S WORT WITH OTHER MEDICATIONS?

A few recent reports have shown that St John's Wort is capable of reducing the blood levels of other medications that are being taken concurrently. This effect arises from the tendency of St John's Wort to increase the amount of certain enzymes produced by the liver to break down chemicals. The list of drugs that can be affected by this interaction is rather long and includes medications for the treatment of cardiac problems, high blood pressure, seizure disorders and HIV infections, oral contraceptives and hormone replacement therapy (HRT), and medications to prevent rejection of transplanted organs. **If you are considering taking St John's Wort and are on any other medications, be sure to consult your doctor before starting the herb.**

HOW LONG SHOULD I STAY ON ST JOHN'S WORT?

This question could just as easily be asked in relation to any other anti-depressant. In one form or another, it is one of the more common questions on the mind of anyone who has felt the benefit of an anti-depressant medication. The relief and gratitude experience is counterbalanced in many people by a sense of unease at having to be on a medication for an undefined and possibly indefinite period of time. The honest answer is that we just can't predict how long someone will need to be on an anti-depressant. If the depression has been a single short-lived episode, it may be possible to stop the anti-depressant after six months of remission without risking relapse. If there is a history of repeated episodes or long-standing depression, however, there is a high likelihood that depression will recur or relapse if the anti-depressant is stopped. In such people it generally makes good sense to stay on an anti-depressant indefinitely. Although there have been no long-term studies of St John's Wort in depression – and I should say that such studies are few and far between for other anti-depressants as well – there is no evidence of any long-term problems in those who have been on St John's Wort for months or even years.

After several months on treatment, people often experiment and stop their anti-depressants just to make sure that they still really need them. If you do this, be sure to watch out for early signs of relapse and return to the anti-depressant as soon as these appear. It is much easier to reverse the symptoms of depression in their initial stages than after they are fully established again.

SHOULD EVERYONE TRY ST JOHN'S WORT?

Our experience with other anti-depressants suggests that the answer to this question is 'no.' Although anti-depressants, as their name implies, improve mood in people who are suffering from depression, there is no evidence that they are universal 'pick-me-ups'. Since St John's Wort appears to work in ways that are similar to those of other anti-depressants, I would expect that it would also be unhelpful for those who are not depressed. In any event, there is certainly no evidence that the herb benefits people who are not suffering from depression. So it doesn't make sense to go to the expense and trouble of taking St John's Wort and risking potential side-effects unless you are not feeling depressed.

IS ST JOHN'S WORT USEFUL IN THE TREATMENT OF ANXIETY?

Anxiety is often one of the symptoms of depression and when it is part of an overall depressed picture, it appears that St John's Wort will help the anxiety along with the other symptoms of depression. Some people, however, suffer from anxiety without exhibiting any symptoms of depression and so far there have been no research studies to determine whether these people will benefit from St John's Wort. It would not be surprising if the herb did prove to be of some value in anxiety since many other anti-depressants have been found to be helpful in the treatment of anxiety disorders. There certainly seems little harm in trying the herbal treatment for a month or two if you are anxious and determining for yourself whether it is helpful to you, but you may want to start with a low dosage and increase it slowly since anxious people may be more susceptible to the symptoms of restlessness reported by some people on St John's Wort.

CAN ST JOHN'S WORT HELP ME TO DEAL WITH TEMPORARY STRESS?

This is an interesting question for which we also have no scientific answers. Nevertheless, several people have told me that they have been helped by the herb when they have used it to help deal with the effects of temporary stress, and it would be surprising to me if many people are not already using it in this way to good effect. Once again, you might want to try the herb for yourself and see if it helps. I deal with this question more extensively in the chapter entitled *Beating the Winter Blues*.

HOW ABOUT USING ST JOHN'S WORT FOR OBSESSIVE COMPULSIVE DISORDER (OCD)?

Once again, there are no data that address this question. In the treatment of OCD, the most effective drugs are those that selectively target, and are most potent in affecting, the serotonin system. Since St John's Wort has a more balanced action across three different neurotransmitter systems, it might prove to be less effective than the selective serotonin reuptake inhibitors, such as Prozac and Lustral, in the treatment of OCD. One type of compulsive behaviour which is very hard to treat is compulsive hair-pulling, also known as trichotillomania. Although there are no studies on the use of St John's Wort for this condition, I have reported on one serious case of it who benefited from the herbal remedy (*see pages 39–49*).

WHAT CAN I DO IF ST JOHN'S WORT DOESN'T WORK FOR ME?

Whenever there is an exciting new treatment, it is natural for people to be hopeful that it will be the answer to their problems, and disappointed if it is not. Remember that even if St John's Wort is not effective for you by itself, it may still have some value in combination with other anti-depressants. Bear in mind, though, that no anti-depressant treatment works for everybody and this must surely be true of St John's Wort as well. Take comfort in the knowledge that there are many other available anti-depressants, some old, tried and tested, some newly arrived and claiming all kinds of advantages, and others yet to appear on the market. It is very unusual not to be able to find some medication or combination of treatments that will help extricate a person from the murky depths of depression. My approach with my own patients is to keep trying different approaches and sooner or later, such attempts are almost always successful.

SHOULD I CONSIDER TAKING PREPARATIONS THAT CONTAIN COMBINATIONS OF DIFFERENT HERBS?

If you look on the shelves of your local health food shop, you will find all sorts of mixtures containing St John's Wort along with other herbal remedies. It has often been mixed with valerian, a mild sleeping medication, and sold as an overall restorative. Such combinations have been marketed for many years. Some of the European studies that have compared St John's Wort with placebo have used preparations that include valerian. St John's Wort has also been combined with the herbal anti-anxiety compound, kava-kava, as well as with any number of other substances such as passion flower extract. Should you consider taking such preparations and do they have any advantage over taking St John's Wort alone?

This kind of question does not pertain only to herbal medications, but to synthetic medications as well, where combinations of different medications are available in a single capsule to provide a number of different therapeutic effects.

Even though I frequently prescribe combinations of individual medications, in practice I almost never recommend pre-formulated combinations. The reason for this is very simple. If different medications are doing different things, you need to be able to alter the dosage of each one individually and wait to observe its effects in order to know how best to proceed. A pre-formulated combination may cause a side-effect, for example, and you would not know for sure which of the medications in the formulation was responsible for it. Reasoning along the same lines, I would discourage the use of herbal combinations. Although some of the other herbal remedies may have beneficial effects in their own right, if they are to be tried I recommend that they be taken individually after you have had a chance to observe the effects of taking St John's Wort by itself. A discussion of the effects of kava-kava and valerian go beyond the scope of this book, but they are herbs with valuable therapeutic potential in their own right and the interested reader is referred to Jean Carper's authoritative and highly readable *Miracle Cures* (HarperCollins, 1997) for a detailed discussion of these herbs and how best to use them.

In summary, herbal mixtures are not recommended. You may well benefit from taking more than one herb, but I recommend that you take each one for a specific purpose, in a specific dosage and only after you have some knowledge about its potential side-effects as well as its potential benefits.

IS ST JOHN'S WORT ADDICTIVE?

There is no evidence that St John's Wort is addictive. I generally recommend that any anti-depressant be tapered rather than stopped abruptly, though I know of no reports of any withdrawal after St John's Wort is stopped. As with any other anti-depressant, however, depressive symptoms may recur when the medication is discontinued.

CAN ST JOHN'S WORT WORK AT FIRST AND THEN STOP WORKING? WHAT SHOULD I DO IF THAT HAPPENS?

It is not uncommon for an anti-depressant that works initially to stop working after a period, which may range from weeks to years. St John's Wort is no exception in this regard and depressive symptoms may recur after an initial response. A relapse of this kind may be due to a worsening of the depression, which is sometimes the result of a definable cause such as a personal loss, a new stress or the onset of winter. Wherever possible, the first-line response to such a setback is to deal with the underlying cause, for example to obtain extra support from friends and family, adopt strategies to help deal with the stress or increase the amount of environmental light, all of which are described in more detail in the previous chapter.

If the trigger for relapse cannot be identified or if the steps to correct it by making environmental changes are unsuccessful, medication adjustments can be made, including increasing the dosage of St John's Wort or adding another anti-depressant. Sometimes a person develops what is known as tolerance to an anti-depressant, which means that certain chemical changes in the brain override the beneficial effects of the medication. In this case it can pay to switch to another medication or to add a medication specifically designed to potentiate the effects of the anti-depressant. Drugs such as lithium carbonate and synthetic thyroid hormone have been reported to be effective potentiators of conventional anti-depressants and may be of value when added to St John's Wort as well. If the medication situation is complicated enough to warrant potentiation of an anti-depressant, it is certainly necessary for a highly skilled doctor to be involved in treatment decisions. The purpose of providing you with this information is so that you can understand some of the steps your doctor is likely to consider in dealing with the delayed development of unresponsiveness to an anti-depressant.

One possible reason why St John's Wort may stop working is that the composition of active ingredients may vary from one batch of St John's Wort to another. You might suspect this to be the case if you purchased a new batch of St John's Wort just before noticing the change in anti-depressant effect. Reliability of quality control is one reason why I recommend the brand of St John's Wort with the best documented and most reliable track record, namely Kira™, so as to minimize the likelihood of relapses due to inconsistencies between batches.

WHAT ARE THE PROS AND CONS OF USING ST JOHN'S WORT VERSUS THE SSRIS SUCH AS PROZAC AND LUSTRAL?

It is important to remember that there have been no head-to-head trials comparing St John's Wort with the SSRIs in the treatment of depression. All reports of comparisons between the herbal and synthetic anti-depressants are therefore anecdotal. Nevertheless, there are lessons to be learned from anec-dotes and one conclusion I have reached, based on many stories such as the ones included in Chapter 12, is that there are certain people who do better on St John's Wort than on the SSRIs. When both types of anti-depressants are used in their conventional dosages, St John's Wort appears to be superior to the SSRIs with respect to side-effects. Particularly, it appears to cause fewer sexual side-effects, less weight gain and fewer feelings of dullness in thinking or feeling. When used in their conventional dosages it is possible that the SSRIs may be more potent and I have encountered cases where they have reversed depressive symptoms that did not respond to St John's Wort alone. In the currently planned multi-centre research study sponsored by the US National Institute of Mental Health, St John's Wort and the SSRI Lustral are to be compared for the first time. It will be fascinating to see how they stack up against each other. In the meanwhile each depressed person will have to choose the type of anti-depressant – herbal or synthetic – best suited to his or her needs based on the information available and his or her own personal preferences.

Appendix

Scale of Well-being

Please mark, with an X, on the scale overleaf the way you feel today: Try to pick the same time of the day each day, then carefully review the whole 24 hours and make your decision. Use as the 'anchor' points the *best* you have ever felt on the right and the *worst* you have ever felt on the left. (Write into the boxes provided what the best and worst mean for you personally.) Try not to let the previous day influence you when you score the next day.

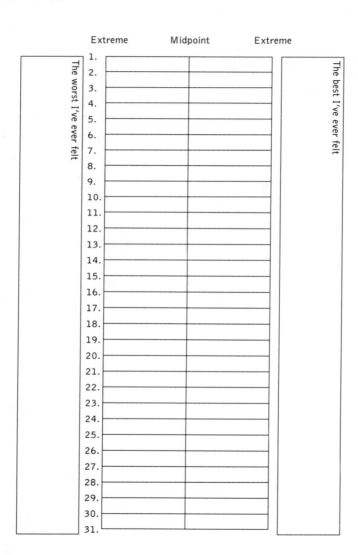

Figure 1

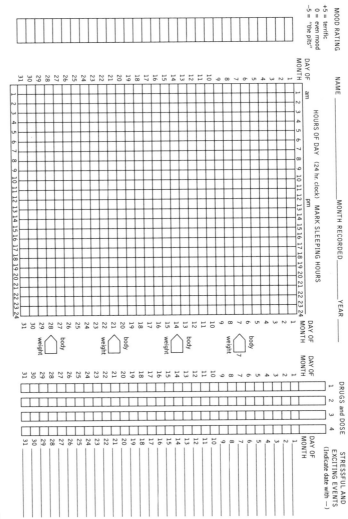

Figure 2:
Mood Log

Useful Addresses

ST JOHN'S WORT

St John's Wort is available from all good health shops.

About Herbal Medicines

Bioforce (UK) Ltd
Dundonald KA2 9BE

Gerard House Ltd
836 Christchurch Road
Bournemouth BH7 6BZ

G Baldwin and Co
171 Walworth Road
London SE17 1RW

American Botanical Council
PO Box 201660
Austin, TX 78720
Fax: 512 351 1924
e-mail: custserv@herbalgram.org
web: www.herbalgram.org

Support Groups

The Manic Depression Fellowship
8–10 High Street
Kingston-upon-Thames
Surrey KT1 1EY
Tel: 020 8874 6550

National Association for Mental Health
Granta House
Broadway
London E15 4BQ
Tel: 020 8519 2122

The Psychotherapy Centre
1 Wythburn Place
London W1H 5WL
Tel: 020 7723 6173

Bibliography and Further Reading

ST JOHN'S WORT

Introduction

American Botanical Council, Commission E Monographs (*see Resources*).

St John's Wort in Everyday Life

Judd, L.L., Rapaport, M.H., Paulus, M.P., Brown, J.L. 'Subsyndromal Symptomatic Depression: A New Mood Disorder?', *Journal of Clinical Psychiatry*, 55 (supplement 4), (1994), 18–28.

Liebowitz, M.R., Gorman, J.M., Fyer, A.J., et al. 'Social Phobia: Review of a Neglected Anxiety Disorder', *Archives of General Psychiatry*, 42 (1985), 729–736.

The Prozac of Herbs

Jacobsen, F.M. 'Fluoxetine-induced Sexual Dysfunction and an Open Trial of Yohimbine', *Journal of Clinical Psychiatry*, 53 (4), (1992), 199–122.

Ross, J. *Triumph Over Fear*. New York, Bantam Books, (1994).

Beating the Winter Blues

Rosenthal, N.E. *Winter Blues: Seasonal Affective Disorder: What it is and How to Overcome it*, New York, Guilford, (1993).

Help for the Elderly

Jenike, M.A. ed. *Geriatric Psychiatry and Neurology*, 7 (supplement 1), October 1994.

History and Mythology

Jones, W.H.S. *Pliny: Natural History*, Cambridge, MA, Harvard University Press, vol 7, (1956).

Gunther, R.T. *The Greek Herbal of Discorides*, New York, Hafner Publishing, (1968).

Guterman, N. *Paracelsus Selected Writings*, New York, Pantheon Books, (1951).

Marzell, H. 'Johanniskraut eine Vokskundlich: Botanische Studie', *Natur*, 10, (1918), 138–140.

Sala, A. *Essentiarum Vegetabilium Anatome*, Germany, Rostock, (1630).

Rogers, T.B. 'On the action of St John's Wort as a Sensitizing Agent for Non-pigmented Skin, *American Veterinary Review*, 46, (1914), 145–162.

Daniel, Dr. med. 'Johanniskraut Bei Psychischen Storungen', *Hippokrates*, 10, (1939), 929–932.

Thornton, R.J. *A Family Herbal*, 2nd ed, London, Crosby, (1814).

Carmichael, A. *Carmina Gadelica*, 1, Norman Macleod, Edinburgh, (1900).

Aubrey, J. *Miscellanies*, London, Edward Castle, (1696).

Vickery, A.R. 'Traditional Uses and Folklore of Hypericum in the British Isles', *Economic Botany*, 35, (1981), 289–295.

Modern Times: Research Findings

Jenike, M.A. ed. 17 relevant articles. *Geriatric Psychiatry and Neurology*. 7, (supplement 1), October 1994.

Linde, K., Ramirex, G., Mulrow, C.D., Pauls, A., Weidenhammer, W., Melchart, D. 'St John's Wort for Depression: An Overview and Meta-analysis of Randomized Clinical Trials', *British Medical Journal*, 313, (1996), 253–258.

Muller, W.E., Kasper, S. eds. 12 relevant articles, *Pharmacopsychiatry*, 30 (supplement 2), September 1997.

Politics and Economics of St John's Wort

Regier, D.A. *et al.* 'The de Facto US Mental and Addictive Disorders Service System: Epidemiologic Catchment Area Prospective 1-Year Prevalence Rates of Disorders and Services', *Archives of General Psychiatry* 50, (1993), 85–94.

Hirschfeld, R. *et al.* 'The National Depressive and Manic-Depressive Association Consensus Statement on the Undertreatment of Depression', *JAMA*, 277 (4), (1997), 333–340.

Brody, J.E. 'In Vitamin Mania, Millions Take a Gamble on Health', *New York Times*, October 26, 1997.

Naisbitt, J. *Megatrends*, New York, Warner Books, (1988).

Okie, S. 'Herbal Relief', *Washington Post*, Health Section, October 14, 1997.

Santiago, J.M. 'The Costs of Treating Depression', *Journal of Clinical Psychiatry*, 52 (11), (1993), 425–426.

Cott, J.M. 'In Vitro Receptor Binding and Enzyme Inhibition by Hypericum Perforatum Extract', *Pharmacopsychiatry*, 30 (supplement 2), 108–111.

Diagnosing Your Own Depression

Jamison, K.R. *An Unquiet Mind*, New York, Knopf, (1995).

Bowlby, J. *Attachment and Loss*, Basic Book, (1967).

Diagnostic Criteria from DSM-IV, Washington D.C., American Psychiatric Association, (1996).

An Anti-depressant Lifestyle

Garber, J. & Seligman, M.E.P. *Human Helplessness: Theory and Applications*, New York, Academic Press, (1980).

Berger, M., Vollmann, J., Hohagen, F., Konig, A., Lohner, H., Voderholzer, U., Riemann, D. 'Sleep Deprivation Combined with Consecutive Sleep Phase Advance as a Fast-acting Therapy in Depression: An Open Pilot Trial in Medicated and Unmedicated Patients', *American Journal of Psychiatry*, 154, (6), (1997),870–872.

Burns, D.D. *Feeling Good: The New Mood Therapy*, New York, Avon, (1992).

Frequently Asked Questions

Burrell, F.A. 'Some Uses of the Oleum Hyperici', *New England Medical Monthly*, 7, (1887), 342–345.

Brown, O.P. *The Complete Herbalist: The People, Their Own Physicians*, (1885).

Schmidt, U., Harrer, G., Kuhn, U., Berger-Deinert, W., Luther, D. 'Interaction of Hypericum Extract with Alcohol', *Nervenheilkunde*, 6, (1993), 314–319.

Carper, J. *Miracle Cures*, New York, HarperCollins, (1997).

Index